Society of Fear

Heinz Bude

Translated by Jessica Spengler

polity

First published in German as *Gesellschaft der Angst* © Hamburger Edition
HIS Verlagsges. mbH, Hamburg, Germany, 2014. This translation from
German is published by arrangement with Hamburger Edition.

This English edition © Polity Press, 2017

The translation of this work was supported by a grant from the
Goethe-Institut.

Polity Press
65 Bridge Street
Cambridge CB2 1UR, UK

Polity Press
101 Station Landing, Suite 300
Medford, MA 02155, USA

ISBN-13: 978-1-5095-1949-1
ISBN-13: 978-1-5095-1950-7 (pb)

A catalogue record for this book is available from the British Library.

Typeset in 11 on 14 pt Sabon by
Servis Filmsetting Ltd, Stockport, Cheshire
Printed and bound in the UK by 4edge Limited

The publisher has used its best endeavours to ensure that the URLs for
external websites referred to in this book are correct and active at the time
of going to press. However, the publisher has no responsibility for the
websites and can make no guarantee that a site will remain live or that the
content is or will remain appropriate.

Every effort has been made to trace all copyright holders, but if any have
been inadvertently overlooked the publisher will be pleased to include any
necessary credits in any subsequent reprint or edition.

For further information on Polity, visit our website: politybooks.com

Contents

v

I will show you fear in a handful of dust.

T. S. Eliot

Preface

If we want to understand a social situation, we must give a voice to people's experiences. The public today is inundated with data on poverty risk rates, the dissolution of the middle class, the increase in depressive disorders, and declining turnout among first-time voters. But what these findings mean and how they relate to one another remains unclear.

There is no question that changes are brewing in the correlation between social structures and individual attitudes. Cognitive psychologists, behavioral economists, and neurophysiologists are therefore turning their attention to the black box of the self, which now has to mediate between these dimensions without the benefit of traditional paradigms or conventional models. The self-help books that are based on their research tout mental activation programs and physical relaxation techniques.

Sociology can play its hand here if it takes itself seriously as an experiential science. Experience is the source of evidence for empirical research and personal life praxis alike. This experience manifests itself in discourse and is based on constructs. But the point of reference for analyzing blog posts, newspaper articles, medical bulletins, or opinion polls must be the experiences that are expressed within them.

One important empirical concept in society today is the concept of fear. In this context, fear refers to what people feel, what is important to them, what they hope for, and what drives them to despair. Fears reveal the direction in which a society is moving, where the flash points are, when certain groups will mentally withdraw, and how doomsday sentiments or resentment can suddenly proliferate. Fear shows us what's wrong with us. Sociologists who want to understand society today must look to the society of fear.

Acknowledgments

I would like to thank Birgit Otte, who had the idea for this book, and Sabine Lammers, who edited the text with a steady hand.

Thank you to my wife, Karin Wieland, who saved me from fixed ideas, as always, and to my daughter, Pola, with whom I discussed the major ideas on our shared streetcar journeys.

Heinz Bude, June 2014

Fear as a principle

In modern societies, fear is an issue that affects everyone. Fear knows no social bounds. The high-frequency trader sitting in front of his computer is just as susceptible to anxiety as the deliveryman returning to his depot, the anesthetist picking up her children from kindergarten, or the model looking in the mirror. In its substance, too, fear is infinite: fear of school, fear of heights, fear of poverty, fear of heart disease, fear of terrorism, fear of losing social status, fear of commitment, fear of inflation. And fear can develop along any axis of time. We may fear the future because everything has gone so well up to this point; we may feel fear in the present because we worry about our next steps, since a decision in favor of one option is always a decision against another; and we may even fear the past if we think that something we've put behind us might rear its head again.

Niklas Luhmann, whose systems theory of functional equivalents always provides for alternatives in any situation, views anxiety as perhaps the only *a priori* principle in modern society about which all members of society

are in agreement. It is the principle that applies absolutely when all other principles have been qualified.[1]
Anxiety can bring the Muslim woman into conversation
with the secularist, the liberal cynic with the despairing
human rights activist.

But no one can convince someone else that their fears
are unfounded. At most, fears can only be contained and
dissipated through discussion. Of course, this requires
that we accept the fears of our interlocutors instead of
denying them. This is a well-known therapy scenario;
recognizing your own fears can make you more open
and flexible, so you do not need to immediately react
defensively and dismissively when fear comes into play.

Though they are obviously diffuse, the fears currently coursing through the public consciousness say
something about a particular sociohistorical situation.
Through concepts of fear, the members of a society
come to an understanding about the conditions of
their co-existence: who moves forward and who is left
behind; where things break and where chasms open up;
what is inevitably lost and what might yet survive. It is
through concepts of fear that society takes its own pulse.

In 1932, on the eve of the Nazi era, Theodor Geiger
published a classic work of social structural analysis
– *The Social Stratification of the German People* – in
which he describes a society dominated by fears of
displacement, loss of prestige, and defensiveness. He
introduces us to the characters typical of the time: the
small businessmen with their burning hatred of social
democratic cooperatives; the homeworkers with their
tiny landholdings who have grown solitary and eccentric on account of their domestic isolation and who tend
toward violent rebellion; the young secretaries with

their bobbed hair who are threatened by rationalization and who dream of dashing gentlemen. There are
also the miners who gain their sense of self-worth by
heroicizing the dangers of their profession, and whose
unionized collective interests are not so much institu-
tionally organized and class-conscious in nature as they
are comradely and professional; the petty bureaucrats
who guard their tiny sliver of power all the more jeal-
ously and flaunt it all the more eagerly the more their
positions are squeezed by pay grades and internal tasks;
the army of young graduates who experience a decline
in the value of their education, the disintegration of
their status, and the exclusivity of the professional
world; and, finally, the various characters from the
capitalist class, between whom there is no love lost: the
large-scale landowners who find capitalism's intrinsic
concept of a global economy unpalatable, the *rentiers*
who have a finger in every pie and no loyalty to any
particular social roots, the captains of industry who, on
account of the relative immobility of their investments,
have been tied to specific industrial sites for generations,
and the resourceful merchants whose chain stores keep
the urban populace stylishly decked out and supplied
with delicacies from overseas – and not forgetting those
who have been unsettled by the global economic crisis,
an irregular class of the unemployed who have nothing
to lose, and for whom nothing of permanence seems to
be of any value.

In the social portrait that Geiger sketched freely but
with lively precision, all of these people were united by
the feeling that the social order from which they came
had been superseded. The world of salaried employees
that emerged from multiple regroupings of the working

class and (in due course) from educated circles, the "old middle class" clinging to its property-owning mentality, and the bourgeoisie of the center collapsing into countless interest groups – none of them found social or political forms of expression with which they could identify, either for themselves or society as a whole. Grizzled old social democracy seemed to be trapped in outmoded ideas, the center appeared more inclusive and encompassing but also had to uphold a Thomist-Catholic social philosophy, and the economic and national liberal parties were reeling just like the social classes and milieus searching for a foothold in the confusion. In a situation such as this, anyone who could pick up on the fears of being overrun, left with nothing, and pushed to the margins, and who could then bundle these fears together and direct them at a new target, could mobilize society as a whole. One year before Hitler took power, Theodor Geiger grasped the vanguard importance of a young generation that was removing itself from history, stylizing itself as an agent of national activism and, in doing so, turning the rumble of fear into the engine of a new age. Today we know that these ranks produced the ideological avant-garde of the totalitarian era, who functioned as the controlling elites of industrial society well into the 1970s in Germany and beyond.[2]

It was Franklin D. Roosevelt, a man admired to this day as a statesman, who put the issue of fear and the strategy of fear absorption on the political agenda of the twentieth century. In his inaugural address as the 32nd President of the United States of America, which he held on March 3, 1933, in the wake of the terrible Great Depression, he found the words that would establish a new type of politics: "The only thing we have to fear is fear itself."[3] Free men must not be afraid of fear because this can rob them of their self-determination. Someone who is driven by fear avoids what is unpleasant, denies what is true, and misses out on what is possible. Fear makes people dependent on seducers, guardians, and gamblers. Fear leads to the tyranny of the majority because everyone runs with the pack; it allows one to toy with the silent masses because no one raises their voice in protest, and once the spark has been ignited, it can throw all of society into panicked confusion. We should take Roosevelt's words to mean that the first and foremost responsibility of national politics is to allay the fears of citizens.

One can view the entire development of the welfare state in the second half of the twentieth century as a response to Roosevelt's claim. Eliminating the fear of disability, unemployment, and old-age poverty is supposed to form the backdrop for a self-confident citizenry – one which explicitly includes employees – so that they are free to organize themselves in order to express their interests, they are free to lead their lives according to their own principles and preferences, and so that, in cases of doubt, they can stand up to the powerful in full awareness of their freedom. As Franz Xaver Kaufmann might put it, politics of fear leads to "security as a sociological and sociopolitical problem."[4]

If you fall, someone should catch you; if you are at a loss, someone should advise and support you; if you are born into disadvantage, you should be compensated. This is why the welfare state of today has taken up the cause of providing qualifications to the under-qualified, advice to people and households in debt, and compensatory education for children from underprivileged families. The purpose of this is not just to combat poverty, social exclusion, and systematic social disadvantage, but to combat the fear of being thrown on the scrapheap, disenfranchised, and discriminated against.

A certain reflexive effect comes into play here. By using the principle of fear as a reference point, the welfare state – with its measures for security, empowerment, and equality – delivers itself up to the world of emotions. Can social security, employment offices that have turned into job centers, or quality assurance agencies for everything under the sun banish our fear of fear? For Roosevelt, coping with fear was the decisive criterion for public happiness and social cohesion. During the election campaign that led to his first victory, he proclaimed that he had looked thousands of Americans in the eye and seen that "they have the frightened look of lost children."[5]

It is important to bear in mind that the development of the welfare state in the second half of the twentieth century was framed by an unprecedented promise of integration into modern society. The expectation here was that anyone who made an effort, invested in their own education, and exhibited certain capabilities would find a suitable place for themselves in society. Social placement was no longer pre-determined by one's origins, skin color, region, or gender; instead, it could be influenced by will, energy, and a commitment to one's own dreams and desires. The fact that chance played a much greater role for most people than goals and intentions was acceptable because it was thought that, despite everything, you would end up in a position that, in hindsight, you could feel you had earned and deserved.

Who still actually believes this? Of course, we live in a modern society that values the positions we have earned rather than those allotted to us. The fact that social inequality persists – as has been confirmed time and again by social structural analyses – changes nothing about this principle.

Most young people, who are convinced that we live in a pyramidal class society in which any movement from a lower to a higher social standing is unlikely, assume that they themselves will make it through somehow. They are referred to as a "lost generation," one which has to hire itself out for peanuts despite having all the best qualifications. They get by, but they don't believe they will have careers involving a gradual rise in status, like that of their parents' generation born around 1965.[6]

After all, there are so many things you can do wrong. You can choose the wrong elementary school, the wrong secondary school, the wrong university, the wrong specialization, the wrong trips abroad, the wrong networks, the wrong partner, or the wrong place to live. This implies that a selection process takes place at each of these transitional points, where some get through but many fall by the wayside. The process starts early and never seems to end. You need a good nose, the necessary cooperative skills, a sober sense of relationships, and a feel for timing. Because the corridors ahead are always wider than those behind you, because the social capital from relationships and contacts is growing ever cheaper for the majority but more expensive for a minority, and because relationship markets are becoming more homogeneous and thus more competitive, an individual's fate is increasingly the expression of his or her good or bad life choices.

This change can be summed up by saying that our mode of social integration is shifting from the promise of advancement to the threat of exclusion.[7] We are no longer motivated to keep striving by positive messages, only by negative ones. This prompts us to worry whether our will is strong enough, our skills are right, our appearance is convincing. Our fears have changed along with the costs. If, at every fork in the road, we face the prospect of ending up with those who are left behind waiting for a "second chance" – because life no longer allows for long hauls, only short hops – then anxiety really is, as Kierkegaard says, "freedom's actuality as the possibility of possibility."[8]

Anxiety springs from the knowledge that everything is open but nothing is meaningless. Our entire lives seem to be on the line at every single moment. We can take detours, take breaks or shift our focus, but these actions must make sense and contribute to the fulfillment of our life's purpose. The fear of simply drifting through life is hard to bear. The stress of anxiety is the stress of the search for meaning, and this cannot be alleviated by any state or society.

Sales are booming for self-help books about availability, emotion, and risk based on findings from cognitive psychology, evolutionary theory, and the physiology of the brain. And the message is always the same: you have to keep your options open, think in scenarios, and seize "good opportunities." You should be wary of overestimating yourself, but you should also avoid indecisiveness. And, in general, learning about the bifurcation of the mind should take away your fear of fear. We have an intuitive system that is responsible for fast thinking and a controlling system that works slowly, gradually, and hierarchically. By switching organically between the two, you can stay fit and flexible in a bewildering life with uncertain outcomes.[9]

But if you stand still, stop learning, and fail to strike a balance, you will quickly become a welfare case. And if, in the end, you can even die well or die badly,[10] as the relevant thanatological literature assures us, then the fear of fear itself becomes a hidden motif in our popular doctrines of what comprises a "good life." And the threat of exclusion – as gently as it is brought home to us, and as wise at it may sound – never ends.

This is not the fear that Roosevelt witnessed in the 1930s, that of "lost children" who place their hopes in the protection of the state and entrust themselves to a "good shepherd"; instead, it is that of wily "ego tacticians"[11] who mistrust the state and mock politicians who behave no differently than they do themselves. It is not the fear of being humiliated and forgotten as a group or collective, but rather of tripping up as an individual, losing one's balance and free-falling, without the parachute of a sustaining environment or a traditional "loser culture,"[12] to finally disappear into social oblivion.

This fits with the universalized attribute of precarity[13] that emerged in the first decade of this century. Precarity suddenly applied not just to employment situations other than the "standard" lifelong, full-time job appropriate to one's qualifications, but also to the generations with uncertain paths from education into employment, partnerships based on ideals of romantic love or single parents living together, the social milieus of those who had been declassed and left behind, and the very nature of socialization processes in general. A precarious social existence is one in which standardized expectations

9

bump up against non-standardized realities. This is the norm today, which is why the demand for role distance and ambiguity tolerance is rising. We apparently accept far more divergence than we once did. But this also makes the division between inclusion and exclusion all the sharper. As long as you can make a case for your sexual, religious, or ethical diversity, everything is fine. But you'll quickly find yourself on the outside if your difference makes no difference to the happiness, color-fulness, or creativity of other people. The fear of fear rears its head as soon as someone's otherwise unremark-able difference fails to resonate or connect with others.

This indicates a change in our experience of fear, one which relates to an epochal shift in our behav-ioral programming. In *The Lonely Crowd* – David Riesman's sociological physiognomy of the behavioral world of the twentieth century, which he published in 1950 together with Reuel Denney and Nathan Glazer – Riesman described how Americans were changing from "inner-directed" people guided by their conscience to "other-directed" people guided by their external contacts. When a population expands and people from rural areas stream toward urban agglomerations, and when science and technology become productive forces of their own kind, then individuals need a firmly anchored behavioral control program that is informed by overarching principles and lends stability to their behavior as the world around them changes. Riesman uses the metaphor of an internal gyroscope that can point in different directions while remaining centered on an internal equilibrium. It is naturally frightening to leave your native behavioral habitat as an emigrant, social climber, or "regional pioneer" in order to make your fortune in a different and unfamiliar world; and it is a sign of courage to believe in the enrichment of your world view and the stability of your values nonetheless. In the language of the European tradition, we would refer to these grand notions as "learning" and "conscience." Inner-directed individuals strive to expand their perspectives and test their conscience. This makes it possible for them to reconcile their adaptation to the foreign with their consolidation of the familiar.

Fear is thus conquered in a vertical mode, so to speak. Individuals must sort out their anxious feelings of disaffection, dispossession, and disembedding for themselves and with their god, as the case may be. Bourgeois confessional literature is full of depictions of disorienting learning experiences and agonizing examinations of conscience. But what beckons is the triumph of individuation that makes the individual – who can come from anywhere and fit in anywhere – into an autonomously acting, socially ascribable person who is identical to himself.[14]

But when population growth declines, the countryside becomes a suburb, and the conquest of the world reaches its limits, then interpersonal relations become tighter and more inescapable, and the self must try to adapt to others and come to terms with them in a "shrunken and agitated"[15] world. Then individuals are no longer rewarded for their obsession with proving themselves, but instead for their ability to adopt the perspectives of others, respond resiliently and flexibly to changing situations, and find compromises through teamwork. The psychological gyroscope that maintains internal equilibrium is replaced by a social radar that registers the signals sent by others. The self becomes a self of others – and then faces the problem of forming an image of itself from the thousands of images reflected back at it.

This is not about the importance of appreciation and affection from one's fellow human beings, which is part of the social nature of the self. Instead, the other-directed person is characterized by a greater sensitivity to contact, which turns the expectations and desires of others into the source of direction for one's own behavior. Such behavior is not regulated primarily by the conventions and manners enforced by external authorities, nor by the norms and values internalized through conflict-ridden personal formative processes, but by the expectations, and the expectations of expectations, that are literally negotiated second by second between the people currently involved in a situation. "Role-taking," as the symbolic interactionists would later say, is "role-making."[16]

By distinguishing between inner-directedness and other-directedness, Riesman wanted to illustrate the "exceptional sensitivity to the actions and wishes of others"[17] exhibited by the normal person of today. This sensitivity conceals a defensive and reactive constitution. The other-directed character feels dependent on the judgment of his peers, allies himself with fashionable trends and prevailing opinions, and, in cases of doubt, prefers to remain silent rather than offend or resist. And in moments of loneliness and fatigue, he feels oppressed and enslaved by the assumed needs and desires of the people around him.

This is the breeding ground for what is referred to in the social sciences as the sensation of "relative deprivation."[18] Comparing yourself to others in a similar situation determines how you feel in the world. These others may be friends, contemporaries, or colleagues. And as we know from the psychology of the conservation of resources,[19] losses weigh far more heavily than gains. What does he have that I don't? How do I come off compared to her? This may relate to money, popular status symbols, or a radiant appearance. The self is geared toward others and goes into a tailspin when it no longer believes it can keep up. We are timid and cautious when we feel abandoned, and we grow stronger and more confident when we believe we can appeal to others and win them over.

The idea of what others think of us, and what they think we think of them, thus becomes a source of social anxiety. It is not the objective situation that weighs on individuals and breaks them down, but rather the sense of losing out compared to significant others. Other-directed characters lack the inner reserves that could make them relatively immune to absurd comparisons and ludicrous temptations. Behind their unbridled envy is a deep fear of not being able to keep up, of being the dupe who is left out and left behind.[20]

This fear is very difficult for other-directed individuals to admit to or share with others, however. It is what drives Willy Loman in Arthur Miller's *Death of a Salesman* and the suburban housewives in Betty Friedan's *The Feminine Mystique*. They prefer to hunker down with their bad feelings, have a bourbon at every opportunity, swallow sedatives like candy, and seek refuge in the crowd with their insatiable need for feedback and belonging. It is no coincidence that David Riesman's book – which captured the social condition of twentieth-century humanity better than any other – is called *The Lonely Crowd*.

All of this raises multiple questions. What do the fears of the "lonely crowd" of today look like? Who makes up the "silent majority" that feels patronized and over-looked? Which social developments make people feel powerless, and when do people feel completely abandoned? And, naturally, how can the self withstand this fear, and which discourses and rituals can help it reach an understanding with others about their shared fears? The phenomenology of fear illustrates the kind of society in which we live.

Longing for a non-terminable relationship

Even love apparently can't dispel fear – although love promises that you will no longer have to fear the other because your beloved partner will catch and cherish your vulnerable self. Nonetheless, for other-directed people, intimate relationships are definitive proof of their assumptions and feelings about the nature of interpersonal existence itself. Personal connections are channeled through a spiral of reciprocal perspective-taking that forms the bridge between the *I* and its *you*. Ronald D. Laing, who analyzed the disturbances and follies in the radar system of the other-directed character, described the process of interpersonal perception as follows:

> What I think you think of me reverberates back to what I think of myself, and what I think of myself in turn affects the way I act toward you; this influences in turn how you feel about yourself and the way you act toward me, and so on.[1]

Two things about this quote are noteworthy. On the one hand, we find an increasingly close and direct process of mutual scanning and synchronization, which makes it almost impossible to determine who started with what. Via channels of interpersonal perception, the self gets a sense of itself as being separate from the other. On the other hand, it is clear that this process only goes on indefinitely because neither of the two partners is ultimately transparent and accessible to the other. Despite the confusion of perspectives, there is an absolute, insurmountable border between the *I* and the *you*. To put it paradoxically: attachment is based on separation.

Post-coital tristesse is the embodiment of this contradiction. The cigarette afterwards – or maybe the bite of an apple these days – is meant to distract from the sense of separation after the fusion. Just a moment ago the lovers were inseparable, now they are strangers lying side by side. For a moment, the question hanging in the air is how it can ever be otherwise. Solitude appears to be the first and last truth of the self.

This momentary awareness of the sadness of existence hits so hard because, in modern societies, nearly all social relationships are subject to dismissal. The right of termination, which can be exercised by either party, certifies the freedom to stay or to go. Employment contracts that have covered half a lifetime are terminated, as are childhood friendships that were expected to last forever, memberships in parties that your mother or father belonged to before you, and even marriages and life partnerships that were sealed at the altar, in the courthouse, or with words of eternal loyalty.

The negative freedom of deliberate termination and willful rejection is the very basis of the freedom of today's self. Saying "no" is its strongest expression of self-agency. Environments and organizations that pro-

hibit the individual from saying "no" are rightly viewed
as robbing people of their freedom and destroying
their identity. Erving Goffman called prisons, monaster-
ies, and psychiatric hospitals "total institutions"[2] that
reduce the self to the role of prisoner, monk, or inmate.

But this insistence on the negative "freedom from"
conceals a hidden desire for the positive "freedom to."[3]
Ahead of any questions about community, this is, first
and foremost, the freedom to attach oneself to a partner.
In an age governed by the ideal of romantic love – in
which the love between the lovers alone, and not the
decorous, instrumental, or otherwise obvious alliances
between the partners' families, is expected to constitute
a bond for life – attachment is a risky business because
the partners cannot know how much tolerance of frus-
tration is inherent in their love for one other. When the
sexual overestimation stemming from the madness of
infatuation fades, the partners must necessarily come
to an agreement on a long-lasting emotional concept
for their partnership. This generally happens through
narratives of getting to know one another and weather-
ing relationship crises, of joint vacations and property
acquisition projects, and, above all, through the endless
narratives (with supporting photographic evidence) of
raising children together.

Since your partner is always the other, even if you
can't imagine being with anyone else – someone who is
a stranger at heart, whose dark thoughts, secret desires,
and bizarre fantasies are hidden from you – you must be
constantly alert. An obsession in the mind of the other
can suddenly put everything up for grabs. When viewed
in this way, loving relationships are based on the fear of
freedom. Both the *I* and the *you* have the freedom to say

"no" (whether for trivial reasons or out of deep disappointment) and thus to take the liberty of leaving the other alone. "We grew apart" is the set phrase explaining a separation – as inadequate as it is accurate.

Even an intimate relationship in which you have surrendered yourself to one another, adapted to one another through interpersonal learning processes, and, ultimately, grown dependent on one another in your shared life can, in principle, be terminated. When this happens and people say their world has collapsed, what they mean is that their self has lost the foundation of the interpersonal relationship they took for granted, whose everyday familiarity conveyed a feeling of ontological security. The fear of this inconceivable break in the bond of love is the basis of the relationship fears that go hand in hand with the modern principle of the terminability of all social relationships.

Every loving relationship is probably subject to such fear. Perhaps free-floating fear is actually the fundament of and prerequisite for an unconditional love that can be neither forced nor stopped. "How do I love thee?" Elizabeth Barrett Browning wrote in 1850 in the most famous of her *Sonnets from the Portuguese* (Sonnet 43) – and the answer is: "Let me count the ways [...] I love thee with a love I seemed to lose." But it is precisely this boundless, ceaseless state of subjection that fills the other-directed character with dread. After all, the other to whom you devote and surrender yourself can also make your life hell. Is love risky because lovers do not merely mutually admit to their "power to do harm"[4] but actually open themselves up to it? There are essentially only two options available to the sensitive self that recognizes its vulnerabilities: right from the start, it can calculate its attachment prospects or it can multiply its attachment expectations. In both cases, skeptical realism is an effective means of overcoming the fear of being left alone.

These days, partnership algorithms can help us find potential partners who fit with us. The respective websites and agencies offer matching methods based primarily on the factor of education. This is because education guarantees mutual connectivity between people looking for a partner, at least when it comes to questions of taste, sociability, and life goals. Someone who likes Blinky Palermo[5] will never fit with someone who loves musicals and Christmas markets, even if both of them bought their kitchens at IKEA. Furthermore, women tend not to form attachments to men who have a lower level of education. Men have traditionally had fewer problems with this, but masculine domination also isn't what it used to be. Men increasingly want to be seen with self-confident women who, like themselves, have plans for their life. The "trophy woman" of today combines sex appeal with sophistication and affection with ambition. Furthermore, education can be combined easily with character traits and problem-solving styles, making it a predictor for the optimal match in a relationship, be it homosexual or heterosexual.

Choosing can make one choosy, of course, and the danger of being choosy is that you might not find anyone at all.[6] The sense of being spoilt for choice comes from an optimization idea: that there could always be someone better out there who promises an even happier, sexier, more successful relationship. The fear of missing the boat is what prompts us to take the person who's left at the end of a friend's party – or, after a few disappointing diversions, to return to a childhood companion.

As we confront the frightening thought that we may never find someone, the truth of probability theory begins to dawn on us – namely, that the tendency in the majority of cases says nothing about the reality of the individual case. What's true in the here and now does not necessarily apply anywhere else. The encounter between *I* and *you*, as we know from philosophers of interpersonal relationships such as Martin Buber,[7] is always immediate and current, but it is also always threatened by a hesitation that is somewhat too long or an approach that is somewhat too fast.

An encounter is not a choice. Obviously, choosing a lover and life partner must be thought of in a different way than choosing an object or a product. The question of whom I should choose necessarily implies the counter-question: who will choose me? If a relationship is going to come out of it, choosing also involves being chosen. I want to be a desirable other for another, just as another should be an attractive other for me. This is quite mysterious because it revolves around the union of two singular beings who demand to be recognized as singular beings. How is it possible to come together in such a way that the *I* becomes a unique and irreplaceable *you* for another? It seems that we must open ourselves up to the coincidence that will bestow upon us a *you* who corresponds to no selection program. This is the original fantasy of romantic love as love at first sight, in any case. Romeo and Juliet see one another and experience a sudden, undying love that defies all social boundaries and rational calculation. In the act of choosing, we must reckon with the prospect of contingency, which means that everything can always turn out differently. The films of Eric Rohmer and the novels of Patrick Modiano deal with aleatoric fantasies of love at the right moment. What ultimately turns out to be fortune or misfortune remains anything but clear. In art, this is where the appeal lies: in episodes that are cut short and picked up again somewhere completely different, nameless faces that refuse to fade from memory, and fleeting encounters mourned by the spirit.

The attempt to calculate our attachment prospects thus ends with the frightening realization that we have no control over the creation of attachments. Psychoanalytical or even psychotherapeutic advice books will tell us that the search grid for our choice of partner can be traced back to our childhood relationship with our mother and father, but this doesn't help us much when we know that our choices are dependent on the choices of random others who are closed off and hidden from us.

The solution proffered by the other-directed self for overcoming this dilemma, which arises from the reciprocity of choice, is to multiply the number of attachment projects. If all social relationships, including intimate and existential ones, are not only threatened by the possibility of termination but are actually terminated on a massive scale – as soaring divorce rates show – then in the interests of self-preservation, it is smarter not to expect everything from a single relationship. The popular notion of a "life-phase partner," with whom one can still interact openly and honestly even after the relationship ends, supports the idea of an invulnerable self who can find a partner appropriate to the respective "development task" in each phase of life. Many a relationship advice book might try to convince us of this, but in reality we know that it's a lie. Life is not a series of shipwrecks that can be written off as important experiences on the journey to self-realization. But how else can we bear the conflict between our desire for attachment and our fear of attachment?

We can take refuge in the only non-terminable relationships that are still available to us: the relationships between parents and children and those between siblings.

Family sociologists[8] tell us that the family of today is child-centered. The focus of the family – or, to put it more broadly, the family-style domestic partnership – is not the kinship system or the partners, but the children. In other words, partners do not commit to each other because they want to carry on the legacy of two families, legitimize their sexual relations, or express their shared love for one another. First and foremost they want the bond with a child, a bond that cannot be terminated by either party.

Parents who are driven to despair by their children because they take the liberty of doing one thing or another cannot be rid of those children, any more than children can be rid of the parents they hate because they feel put upon and abused or because they are victims of violence. Desperation, which always sees a way forward, is a tie that binds – and hate, which leads to the total loss of contact, binds even more. Once you are a parent, you will always be a parent, even long after your children have left home and started their own families, just as you will always be a child to your own parents, even after they have grown old and confused. "Blood is a very special juice"[9] – it binds us even in separation, and it outlasts death.

Attachment is the scarce resource supplied by a child. Children are needed not so much as cooperative family members than as commiserating partners. Systemic family analyses reveal how this can affect the relationship dynamics in a family. Children often become contested allies in the rivalry between their parents. They can become a partner substitute in the mind of one parental unit, they can function as the image of all that is good and beautiful or as the scapegoat for all that is ugly and bad, and they can even serve as the figure upon which the mother or father projects their ideal self.[10] This happens in two-parent and single-parent families alike. Single parents who have settled down with their offspring can still keep themselves open to a partner, while two parents living together can each withdraw into their own shells with their unfulfilled partnership desires. The outward forms of so-called happy family life are the same everywhere. What makes such a life special and unique are the relationship twists that arise from unconscious role attributions. In this emotional respect, parents and children are on the same level in a child-centered family.

The threat of termination intensifies the desire for attachment. What can be done about the fear of ending up alone, with no one to share your life? For the other-directed self, relationships between parents and children and between siblings carry the anthropological weight of a natural attachment that cannot be broken by any form of termination, either through mental caprice or mutual agreement.

It seems that the self cannot get by without attachment. But attachment is frightening because the freedom of the self becomes dependent on the freedom of the other. The formula for this paradoxical situation is free-dom through entanglement. I can only want you if you want me, but I can never know whether you really want me – just as you can't know whether I want you with all my heart. Sometimes I don't know it myself. For its own sake, the self can never flee from this fear. The longing for a non-terminable relationship ultimately only proves what it is intended to conceal.

Unease with one's own type

The classic fearful character type in modern societies is the male social climber. We immediately think of the robust go-getters who have grown rich and gotten ahead as property developers, the owners of chain stores, or the directors of agencies for insurance and financial products. They are widespread and often appear in the yellow press in reports about mansions with many rooms, hereditary friendships, and charity events. They also take the form of local princes running medium-sized businesses, special clinics, and law practices.

The make no bones about the fact that they come from humble backgrounds where they were never exposed to the fine arts or rare red wines, but they also leave no doubt that with a willingness to learn, assertiveness, and an understanding of human nature you can make something of yourself. They act down to earth, they cultivate friendships, and they love definitive gestures. And the public is always eager for news from behind the scenes which proves that such social advancement has come at a steep price. No one would be surprised to hear that the wife in the miniskirt who heads off to the stud farm every day no longer has much use for her husband, who is hardly ever home, or that the "self-made man" is concealing the fact that he has a poor brother living on welfare. The road out of nothingness must be paved with bodies.

None of this is hidden from the social climber. As friendly and accepting as the people around him may be, he feels he is under continuous observation as a character type. And this is not the gaze of a political crowd that monitors the credibility of its representatives, nor that of the celebrity crowd that practically expects the objects of its attention to engage in certain escapades; instead, it is that of the crowd of people who have remained at the bottom instead of managing to advance. The social climber believes they are just waiting for the generosity they construe as showing off to become his downfall, for the good friends he has fostered and financed to drop away from him in a crisis, and for he himself to be revealed as a trickster and deceiver in his professional life.

The social climber thus lives in fear of those he has escaped and whose status fatalism he has belied. He knows, of course, that his success is not due solely to his own efforts, that luck or a mentor played a part, or simply that an economic boom played into his hands and gave people such as himself a chance. With the host of others breathing down his neck, he feels guilty in a vague, inexplicable way. He has a sense of having betrayed his origins, and as a result – though, like Max Weber, he considers himself absolutely "unmusical" in matters of religion – he fears the vengeance of the gods.

Certain sights affect him so much that, in such

moments, he thinks everything he achieves and indulges in serves only to drown the fear that makes him so unsettled and driven. The status symbols that are meant to show what he has accomplished then seem insipid and ridiculous to him. At times like these, he can easily tip over into a sentimentality that resembles an apology addressed to no one in particular.

On the other hand, the social climber is under no illusions that, once he has arrived, he will ever be anything more than a tolerated stranger. Even if his daughter earns a good business degree and his son studies experimental film at renowned schools in the UK and USA, he will always have the whiff of the arriviste about him. He is still plagued by the feeling of swimming against the current instead of with it. For this reason, he is continually tempted to succumb to ruthlessness, cunning, and scheming. He will be celebrated as long as he can maintain his position, but if he slips up, he thinks he will have to brace himself for kicks and blows.

The social climber as we know him, from the age of industrial expansion, is a character type caught between two stools. He wants to be neither where he is nor where he came from. It is this positional inconsistency that fills him with dread. He has no idea where to lay his weary head in moments of weakness, so he feels that he has been left entirely to his own devices.[1] It is obviously impossible to enthuse endlessly about one's own power of self-assertion. The status seekers, as Vance Packard called postwar social climbers back in 1959,[2] want to wind up somewhere and belong somewhere. The sociological theory of reference groups[3] has put a name to this desire: people must at least have an imaginary group to which they can relate and which gives them a feeling of belonging and importance. Heroicizing the position of being somewhere in between is not a sustainable strategy. The hard law of social esteem says that those who are unhappy are in the wrong.

The mass phenomenon of social advancement takes on a very different character in our society. The "self-made man" is merely the spectacular version of a general type. We're talking about longer social ascents through generations here: the grandfather who was born in a village and worked his way up on the railroad from a trackman to a locomotive engineer; the son who graduated from a technical college and became managing director of a non-profit housing association; and the granddaughter who earned a doctorate in modern history and is now a professor at an elite university. Many families can tell such tales of advancement, and they are usually evidence of the growing involvement of women in educational and professional life.

For all of their personal efforts, the protagonists of these stories are in tune with a social trend which has made it easier to advance professionally and improve one's personal status thanks to the opening up of the education system and expansion of the employment system. The grandchildren of the great postwar development generation find themselves in a new world of employees and civil servants, one in which they view themselves as leaders but certainly do not think of themselves as alpha types who have to prove themselves at the expense of others.

Two things are important for this predominant type: first, their path through educational institutions that have opened their doors to new groups and classes, and second, their work in professional contexts where communication and representation are expected as key qualifications. The central socialization effect of secondary schools and universities is to drill into their students that performance motivation is the prerequisite for success. These institutions cool down and direct their students' drive to advance by focusing on educational goals. It is common knowledge that teachers give grades not just for formal performance but also (and especially) for the informal internalization of what is taught. Young adults are expected to learn how to participate, express themselves, and generally cut a good figure.

These traits are demanded and valued in careers involving systems analysis, services, and research. The ones who will get ahead are those capable of collegial cooperation, open communication, and probably creative individuality. These are at least necessary, if not always sufficient, conditions in the competition for coveted positions.

If nothing else, it is clear that the ruthless assertiveness of the go-getters described earlier is not an advantage when it comes to this kind of advancement. In regimes of teamwork and project development, one must be more restrained, compliant, and compatible. So the question is not just "what do I think I'm capable of?" but, first and foremost, "how can I convince others that my capabilities will benefit the working group, the department, or the whole company?"

It apparently makes a big difference whether social climbers feel they can move freely or only along set pathways – whether they cast everything outwards or instead seek connections and heed job postings. In one case they fear being undercut and discarded, in the other they fear being overlooked and disregarded.

The social climber who has banked on a corporate career that was not predictable but also not improbable cannot flaunt his fear. He is just one of many who took advantage of an opportunity and got ahead. There will always be others of the same age and with the same background who did not make it – but that's no reason to think you're braver, smarter, or better than them. Everything just happened to fall into place.

The fear scenarios of our perfectly normal social climbers from the baby-boomer generation, the financial crisis generation, or the internet generation are much more deeply buried and concealed. They spring to mind like flashbacks in dreamy situations of evenly suspended attention – when you've woken up too early, or when you hear an old pop song.

Scenes from school in particular are often scenes of fear – the fear of not even making it past the enrollment process, for example. Picture your mother waiting outside in the hallway to hear the results of your school aptitude test. As a six-year-old, you're asked to draw pictures, tell the time, and judge the relative lengths of different sticks. This remains in your memory as an ambiguous situation because it's impossible to determine what is expected and what is being tested.

The terrible feeling of shame returns when, as a ten-year-old, you visit the home of a classmate and drop a fragile teacup filled with clear lime flower tea, which smashes on the floor. Much later, you'll read in a work of classic literature that the plump oval sponge cakes served by your schoolmate's mother, with a look that promised wonders, were called *petites madeleines*.

And then there will be the memory of the overwhelming fury directed at a fellow college student who had simply bluffed when a legendary professor asked him what he thought about the connection between Freud and Piaget after a seminar. The student hadn't done the reading himself, you had just told him about it over lunch, and yet he could blather so cleverly and wittily. And then the professor had taken his leave without so much as a glance in your direction.

Scenes such as these illustrate the fears of the social climber in an upwardly mobile society, as educational opportunities expand and growing value is placed on employment structures. It is the fear of not living up to standards that are impenetrable to you.

What can I expect from the socialization mechanisms of the educational system? How should I behave in distinguished circles? How can I show what I'm capable of? Social climbers always feel they are in foreign territory; they always have to learn how things work first, and nothing is ever relaxed and easy. The fear of inadequacy never abates.

Even something as banal and commonplace as small talk over dinner can become a complicated undertaking. When you can tell from the looks of others that no volley of witticisms is required around the table, you might just want to give up entirely. How does one manage to play this friendly, attentive, none-too-serious ping-pong game in which everyone seems to feel comfortable? The necessary combination of alertness and aplomb simply seems out of reach.

Expanding on the categories developed by Talcott Parsons for role-learning within the family,[4] we could perhaps say that, first, social climbers grow up with a feeling of inadequacy because they always sense that something is expected of them that they cannot provide;

second, they are struck with a feeling of awkwardness because, when dealing with people who are better educated and better situated by birth, they cannot shake the feeling that they are putting their foot in it and making mistakes; and third, they are dominated by a feeling of injustice in all of their efforts and labors because they are quickly overcome by the feeling that they have been treated unfairly and robbed of their due. It is the resulting oversensitivity that causes so many perfectly normal social climbers to make life so hard for themselves.

This applies not only to the standards of one's education and career, but even more so to the standards of one's lifestyle and self-presentation. Because they have gradually distanced themselves from their origins, they can no longer stylize themselves as people from the bottom of the heap. Sweaty pushiness suits them no more than boastful cleverness. The grandfather is usually the reference point for the family's social ascent, and even the father and mother were ambitious enough to move forward and have a better life. So for the grandchildren, this background merely represents deprivation, not origination. For this large group of social climbers, advancement has changed – in psychoanalytical terms – from a category of active projection into one of fearful introjection. To be defeated is something fundamentally different than to fail. This fear is much more fine-grained, but it is also absorbed more deeply in the pores.

On no account does the social climber want to appear narrow-minded, provincial, or stressed. But cosmopolitanism, ease, and self-confidence are not so easy to learn. This is the source of the deep-seated alarm we feel when we see how casually and tastefully someone can decorate a home, how affectionately and purposefully they can raise their children, and how they can be so mindful and disciplined toward themselves. How do the others manage to do what we can't? We cling to the small fears of big spaces and narrow corridors in order to avoid the big fear we feel for ourselves. The door to fear can only be opened a crack, because in the room beyond that door, the walls recede and the floor drops away. But this existential tactic can be even more deadly to the self because, despite all of the yoga classes, coaching sessions, and wellness weekends, the feeling of inadequacy never disappears.

While the old-style social climber fights against a crowd of others whom he believes want to see him brought low, the new social climber quarrels with himself because, for him, the journey is the destination.

Both types are united in their acceptance of self-mobilization and social change, but also in their hopeless desire to be someone else, people who simply are the way they are and who find fulfillment in what they have achieved. The loss of the behavioral habitat of their birth has relegated them to a self with no filling, so they seek a framework for their lives. At the same time, there is tremendous energy in these lives driven by the unease with one's own type. The frequently invoked tendencies toward the individualization of one's self-image and the pluralization of social milieus have their basis in this. This is why political parties that gave a voice to these forces of awakening and transgression – one with the conservative or social-democratic accent of "new centrism" – became a defining feature of the "thirty glorious years" of growing prosperity and peace following World War II. For the large group of social climbers in particular, they transformed the fear of not belonging anywhere into the pride of representing the new world.

When the winners take
it all

In the middle of the manic 1990s, the American economists Robert H. Frank and Philip J. Cook published a
book with the ABBA-inspired title of *The Winner-Take-
All-Society*. The capitalist utopia was undergoing an
incredible revival at the time, as the birth of the web,
advancements in biotechnology, and the assertion of the
global financial market hinted at a real revolution in the
opportunities offered by triumphant capitalism. If you
were quick, shrewd, and bold, you could catapult yourself from nothing into a place in the front row. Dormant
fantasies and desires were roused by hedge-fund managers such as John Paulsen, bio-entrepreneurs such as Craig
Venter, and entrepreneurs working out of their garages
such as Steve Jobs.

The book's subtitle, however, was fairly sobering:
*Why the Few at the Top Get So Much More Than
the Rest of Us*. The explanation provided by the two
economists was, to put it briefly, that we have all been
deceived, because more and more people are competing for fewer and fewer positions, for which higher and

higher prices are being paid. We're familiar with this from the media-backed superstar systems in the worlds of sports, cinema, and the fine arts. Usain Bolt, Angelina Jolie, and Gerhard Richter attract nearly all of the attention, esteem, and income, meaning that there is almost nothing left for the majority of equally distinguished athletes, actors, and painters. Who can name the other 100-meter sprinters from Jamaica, or the co-star of a hit film from France, or the highest-paid living German illustrator?

Frank and Cook believe this type of market is spreading to other areas of modern society. What was previously restricted to the entertainment and luxury markets of sports, film, and art now applies to the markets for lawyers and doctors, investment bankers and corporate consultants, schools and universities, charitable foundations and non-governmental organizations. In each case, small differences in presentation lead to big differences in reputation and payment or profit.

The rhetoric of ratings supports the logic of the market. Rankings are generated for all kinds of questions: which female writer has won the most awards, which actress receives the highest fee per day, and which female CEO has had the most children. The rankings are presented to the public in attractive charts with digitally processed portraits.

Performance is the magic word.[1] To gain social prestige, people must draw attention to themselves in some way. This means they have to combine familiar role elements in a way that enables them to make a striking appearance before an attentive audience. You can make yourself seem particularly interesting through unusual combinations that add a surprising facet to a conventional pattern: an investment banker with a migration background and a backpack, a professor from an educationally disadvantaged background in a Jil Sander suit, a carpenter with a college degree in a hipster outfit. The combination mustn't appear random or overblown, of course; it must create a harmonious image that holds out the prospect of innovative capability and success.

When there are many people competing for a few top spots, selecting the best involves a degree of performance pressure. It is not enough to provide proof of a traditional entrance requirement such as an academic degree, habitus security or, if that's too much to ask, a declaration of loyalty. You have to offer something extra that makes you appear more clever, dazzling, and daring than the rest of the drab crowd. After all, "the winner takes it all!" is a merciless motto.

This isn't really a new phenomenon. Even the classic performance principle[2] in sociology drew a distinction between performance competence and success competence. Performance is only valued and will only lead to social advancement if it is visible and recognized as such. An unknown painter will die as an anonymous hobbyist if he is not discovered and held up as a great artist by a gallerist, critic, or collector. The same applies to an eccentric old inventor who never finds an investor, or a willful discoverer whose pioneering article is never published.

Effort alone is no guarantee of success,[3] not even if the educational system has tucked a prestigious degree in your pocket. Labor markets are geared toward educational qualifications, but they demand that individuals submit to additional selection procedures in their professional lives. A certificate is of little use in a corporate environment or for someone who is self-employed. You must be able to assert yourself in competitive situations without formal criteria; you can't simply harp on about what you were once recognized for in the past. To put it bluntly: the hierarchical educational system monitors performance, while the competition between equals rewards success.

And yet we still believe that success depends to some degree on performance. We're just not sure what kind of performance ultimately determines success. The formula that performance pays off merely conceals the actual ambiguity of the situation. If, in case of doubt, the illusion of performance is what determines whether you're still in the game or you should just fold, you might start to wonder whether success itself is ultimately the only deciding factor. Nothing is more successful than success, as the ones who lose out are always told.

Am I one of the people in the limelight, someone who is admired and who attracts others – or do I have to count myself among the rejected and defeated, those who are thanked for their participation but who have to make do with whatever is left over?

The question that arises here, which is more than just sociologically enlightening, is how the mood of a society is affected when such "winner-take-all" markets spread to every imaginable aspect of social life – that is, when it is not just the markets for the upper echelons that are constituted in this way, but also the markets for mid-range positions, or even the marriage and attention markets that are relevant to everyone. Entertainment programs that let the audience choose the best singer, dancer, or model give us a taste of this, as do the coolly self-promotional conversational styles that are typical of social networks. Wherever we look, there is a social divide between the few who call the trump and dominate the game and the many who can do nothing more than play along and hope to take a trick.

Frank and Cook are appalled by the society of top bonuses, blockbusters, and best-sellers that they believe is destroying the middle-class society from which we come. But they have little to say about what it feels like to live in a "winner-take-all" world. How do the losers who are resigned to the leftovers feel, and how do the winners feel who have taken it all?

Success remains true to the successful for as long as they can convey an impression of success. The certainty of victory eliminates all doubt. Customers eagerly await the latest product models, colleagues applaud shrewd deals, and lenders don't want to miss out on the next big catch. Hence the great astonishment when it subsequently emerges just how long people stood by someone successful, even though the signs of failure had long been impossible to ignore.

This is why winners are usually their own worst enemy when they win. The doubts of others are immediately stoked when signs of self-doubt become apparent in the victor. Public navel-gazing, confessing to bad judgments, and withdrawing from attacks are all toxic. The public quickly starts to feel deceived and betrayed when the stars of the market waver and falter. The respective stock market listings react immediately, and suddenly there are rumors of bad luck in the air.

The winners who take it all are allowed to appear generous, they can show sympathy for the weakness of others, and they should even reveal their humanity when the appropriate opportunities arise – but they must also express their conviction that they dominate the field. Trust is good, but everyone knows that control is better.

The main fear of the winners is a loss of control over their field of rivals. In top positions you have to cooperate, form coalitions, and keep a check on colleagues who are on the same level as you; but the fear here relates chiefly to the danger emanating from people on your team whom you may not even view as competitors. The nervous boy who always has that glint in his eye in stressful situations, the ambitious young woman who seems to be storing away her experiences for her next female boss, or the eternal deputy you inherited from your predecessor – any one of these people might be plotting day after day to trip you up in the phrasing of a final report or a project presentation for the CEO so they can steal the limelight for themselves. The bad thing is that you don't know whether it's true, but you have to take it into account.

The defeated can only dream of such anxious fantasies. They are ruled instead by the poison of resentment. This is a buried feeling of rancor stemming from the fear of their own aggression. Powerless to take revenge, incapable of retaliating, and prevented from a reckoning, they are seized by a mentality which, as Max Scheler put it, is "caused by the systematic repression of certain emotions and affects which, as such, are normal components of human nature."[4] They rail against the regime of unscrupulous locusts who are totally indifferent to the fate of the workers, and they mourn the good old days of industrial paternalism; they bemoan the devastation wrought by a mass culture of fashion and fast-food chains, and they attend vinyl nights and collect illuminated editions of books; they revolt against the capitalism on credit of private deficit spending and dream of a full-reserve economy of honest businessmen.

This feeds a sense of grievance that finds reason for complaint everywhere. They are, like "most of us," the ones who have fallen behind in the scrum for the few positions at the top. Resentment literally means to re-sense a past injury, defeat, or degradation – and there is always a fear of being totally contaminated by this gnawing feeling.

In Theodor W. Adorno's study of the "authoritarian personality," which was produced with Else Frenkel-Brunswik, Daniel Levinson, and R. Nevitt Sanford, Adorno attributed resentment to a rebellious impulse against a system of life that has become impossible and obstructed. One must assert the rebel within one-self in order to be able to identify in any way with the existing system. And the system of selection in the winner-take-all society is outweighed by the fact that inferior characters can reach the top and take everything. One characteristic of the "usurpation complex"[5] is a hatred for winners who are the same as you. If they were "alpha" types against whom you never stood a chance, then you could put your mind at ease. But when faced with so many duds calling the shots, the losers who wind up with nothing fly into a rage. They hate the system, democracy, and capitalism in equal measure.

Sociology has a long tradition of resentment toward *ressentiment*,[6] one which, following Nietzsche, is played out between men of sovereignty and men of resentment. While the man of resentment is characterized by anxiety, pettiness, and doggedness on account of his inhibited revenge, the "noble man" has vanquished the fear of his great desires and liberated himself from the "spirit of revenge."

From a psychoanalytical point of view, Nietzsche's "war against shame" can be identified as the source of his devastating critique of resentment.[7] Those who lose out to a societal trend are filled with shame at their defeat and destined to succumb to self-poisoning through a soul that "squints," as Nietzsche puts it. They always see what is awry, unsuccessful, and obstructed first, and in doing so they rob themselves of happiness out of a fear of their own feelings.

We can accept the winner-take-all society as an honest description of the expansion of the capital-ist principle of the ruthless selection of elites, and we can even praise it as a way of discovering outstanding performers. But this total mobilization of competitive energies comes at a social cost – namely, the prolif-eration of a post-competitive embitterment disorder[8] among the second- and third-place competitors who view themselves as humiliated losers. Their swallowed revenge motif manifests itself in a loss of drive, a ten-dency to withdraw, and an attitude of being offended by life itself. They just wanted a place in the sun like everyone else, but instead they were passed over, embar-rassed, and rejected. All of this lodges so deeply and so firmly because those who were eliminated and passed over feel that the fundamental assumptions of fair play have been violated.

When it comes to socially important competitions, one person can't take it all. Just as schools have grading scales, there are always top, middle, and lower ranks. Even those who are out for victory must have a shot at a recognized midfield position. A performance society needs a culture of success that rewards the winners without demeaning the losers. Otherwise the fear of losing out will only produce resignation and bitterness.

The status panic of the middle class

In accordance with this, fear forms the reality of the soul in the middle strata of our society. Fear afflicts those who have something to lose, who have an idea of what can happen if you make the wrong decision, who feel insecure in their position on the social ladder, and who are familiar with the fear of fear. Looking at it the other way around, however, this would mean that those who have nothing to call their own, who have no choices, who feel they are in the dark anyway, and who have nothing to leave to others are not dominated by the kind of fear that makes you feel guilty even though you are entirely innocent. The fear that is surrounded by blissful innocence is very different from the fear rooted in a feeling of guilt for no apparent reason. While the former fear – that of a child, as Kierkegaard said – involves "a seeking for the adventurous, the monstrous, and the enigmatic,"[1] the latter is contradictory because its apparent gratuitousness and superfluity is the origin of its terrible truth: it is actually the fear of nothing in particular and nothing concrete. It is based on the "anxious possibility of *being able*"[2] and is therefore the fear for oneself.

Is this type of fear a luxury problem that befalls societies when people are doing better, when an expanded middle class offers more life opportunities, and when relatively privileged groups have enough time to think about themselves and their place in the world? Of course not. The idea that material pressure and social seclusion can protect you from the fears of the hyper-nervous and highly secure has, at least since the age of Leo Tolstoy and John Ruskin, been part of the middle-class vision of a redemptive "simple life" – but it has little to do with the reality of lower-class fears. So why is the middle-class world of a today a world of fear? The long period of peacekeeping, prosperity, and guaranteed security after World War II has turned the middle classes throughout the OECD world into a zone of civilizing comfort, social safeguards, and personal development – at least as measured against the class-based societies of the first half of the twentieth century, in which the bourgeoisie and proletariat, the blue-collar and white-collar workers, the middle class and lower classes were still rather brusquely opposed to and alienated from one another, and no one could be certain how the class conflict would play out. The totalitarians of the twentieth century thus sought to use macroviolence and everyday terror to create a sense of certainty that was intended to exorcise the fear of a future filled with social conflict.

Today the smoldering class conflict is no longer an issue.[3] The middle class is dominated by the "unsubstantial non-class" of white-collar workers, as Ulrike Berger and Claus Offe put it in 1984 in their semi-wistful, semi-relieved recollection of the lost world of the class conflict.[4] The middle class is no longer composed solely of the traditional male and female salaried employees – the "NCOs of capital,"[5] as Siegfried Kracauer called these social eunuchs in his classic work of social reportage from 1929 – who labor away in accounting, transportation, and claims offices, or departments for job design, business organization, and corporate development. In societies such as ours, the middle class also encompasses engineers and technicians in research and development centers and, above all, experts in the export-oriented high-productivity economies of automotive manufacturing, the machine tool industry, and plant engineering. The mid-level and high-ranking civil servants in the apparatus of state and the freelancers in the financial services industry, health care, and law enforcement must also be counted among the middle class, of course. This is, therefore, a diverse ensemble of highly qualified and productive employed and self-employed people who pay the majority of taxes, amplify their entitlements through the welfare state, make their voices heard in the electorate – and are the target of advertising for long-lasting comfort goods such as eco-friendly cars, confidently stylish home furnishings, and vacations that are appropriate to their age and family status. They are concerned with care in their old age, income growth in their middle years, learning for the future, and inheritance in the succession of generations.[6] And the technologies of the self[7] – comprising personal responsibility, the pursuit of independence, and time autonomy – are taken as a given.

This is the stylistically influential and power-backed "majority class" in our society which, according to Ralf

Dahrendorf, is made up of people "who belong and can therefore hope to realize many of their aspirations without fundamental change."[8] Why should fear be running rampant among the members of this majority class, of all people? Is there something wrong with this terminology now? Is the majority class no longer a majority? Or do the individual aspirations of its members no longer fit with existing social structures? What is there to fear if the entire social system is ultimately geared toward your way of life?

Throughout the OECD world, from France, to the UK, to the Netherlands, to Italy and Spain – not to mention the USA and Russia – the middle of society seems to be unraveling. In all of these countries there are groups of people who, thanks to the changes in value preferences over the past 30 years of "neoliberalism," have made tremendous gains and, in doing so, have stirred up middle-class conditions that had become consolidated over a long period of redistribution and equalization. The publicly funded townhouses built for lower-middle-class families in the 1930s and 1950s have, since the 1990s, had their walls knocked through and lofts converted to create bright, open, airy spaces for the clientele of the "creative class." Areas where aspiring but not particularly wealthy families once lived have been taken over by young urban professionals from the worlds of finance, fashion, art, consulting, and the internet.

The original residents, at least those who weren't seduced by the incredible boom in property prices, have found themselves rubbing their eyes in disbelief at the sight of all the florists, couriers, fitness trainers, cleaners, kitchen remodelers, and yoga teachers disappearing into the houses of the newcomers. All over the world we find these smart, slick types – with their 4x4s, their mountain bikes, their slow food and numerous children – who show us how to take what the new age has to offer, and who give little thought to those who are left behind. Ralf Dahrendorf called them the new global class with the three Cs of competency, contacts, and concepts, who view crises as opportunities and feel no compunction about taking advantage of structural collapse.[9] They are more at home in the priority areas of international airports than in any native country, they speak English just as well as their mother tongue, and despite the depression they might feel sitting in front of their hotel minibar at night, they see no alternative to the globalization of the economy, law, politics, and sports.

They are also the inventors of online stores, partners in law firms, and the founders of marketing agencies. We don't have to like these contemporary characters, but it seems somewhat excessive to claim that they've dug the grave of middle-class society. We could actually say that, on the contrary, these new entrepreneurial activists have injected fresh energy and a different way of thinking into this society. Winemakers are a good example of how a profession rooted in the "old middle class" can completely reinvent itself by being open to more sophisticated methods of production, different nuances in taste, and new strategies in advertising. The male and, notably, female successors to established family businesses have used their knowledge of the world, their willingness to experiment, and their vintner's craftsmanship to bring about a veritable revolution in quality and prestige here.

All the same, it is impossible to deny the tendencies toward division in the middle class. These initially have to do with the change in employment risks and status opportunities, just like everywhere else. Engineers are in demand all over the world. The situation is different in the insurance sector or the banking industry, where employment is inexorably declining on the whole – with the share of executives in particular shrinking considerably, while mathematics experts are growing more important. Seasoned lawyers or business administrators who have managed to retain their positions now have to consult with young mathematicians who aren't even familiar with the industry in order to find out which financial products have a future in the market and which don't. It's not just that jobs have become scarce here, it's that status has become precarious. In this case, the image of fear slowly creeping up the office towers is a fitting one.[10]

Senior insurance and banking executives share this feeling of precarious privilege with leading newspaper journalists who believe they are working in a doomed industry. The web has robbed them of their information privilege; the free newspapers sprouting up everywhere are siphoning away their buyers; and magazine journalism, which is prospering with well-told stories and artfully arranged images, is already a crowded field.

In general, middle-class earnings are not continuing to rise inasmuch as gains among higher earners have decreased and losses among moderate earners have increased. However, for higher earners in particular, the sometimes sizeable growth in gross earnings has not necessarily resulted in a noticeable improvement in income on account of the comparable growth of taxes and duties. The difference between gross and net income has become much greater for this group than for society on average, which is why their general satisfaction is always shot through with anger. They would immediately subscribe to the notion that honesty doesn't pay – and anyway, they think they pay enough taxes as it is.[11]

The data based on disposable income points to an increase in precarious situations and vulnerable careers among the middle class. These days, who dares does not necessarily win. The threshold is the nine employees you hired to make your own business idea a reality. The numbers say nothing about whether this works better in manufacturing or manual trades than in service sectors such as consulting, organization, teaching, development, or design – but those who want to get by on their own will often lose out.

Freelancers without employees of their own usually work on a fee basis in the shadow of the welfare state as assistant educators, consultants, or social workers. They swing from one fixed-term contract to another or continually write new project proposals. They usually have academic qualifications and have opted to secure their livelihood through entrepreneurship, either out of necessity or desire. Think of the family support worker with a teaching degree, or the mediator who has passed a state law exam, both of whom are now scraping along as solo contractors in the big city. It is not their level of education nor their passion for design and development that separates them from their successful peers with flourishing practices for coaching university graduates or big offices for managing joint building ventures – it's just that they bet on the wrong horse. There are hordes of trained architects who have never earned money in their profession, more than a few licensed pharmacists who have gone bankrupt, and a significant but difficult-to-quantify number of general practice lawyers in places such as the City of London who are just keeping their heads above water with run-of-the-mill cases. The number of people who don't earn enough to live, much less to die, is increasing. This includes not only hairdressers, kiosk owners, and barkeepers, but also lawyers, architects, freelance artists, translators, and university lecturers. With this kind of income, provisions for sickness or old age are almost out of the question. This is where the "fear of undervaluation" is concentrated, which Theodor Geiger, in his famous article from 1930, viewed as the basis of the "panic in the middle class."[12] Anger, hate, and resentment arise when people worry that they have not been awarded the social status they deserve based on their education and qualifications. This claim is asserted all the more stubbornly the less one's current social and economic situation satisfies the craving for recognition that one deems to be legitimate.

Today we refer to this as the "precarious prosperity"[13] that affects people in the middle of our society who could just as easily have wound up in the saturated upper stratum of the middle class. The "potential for self-construction" that is mentioned in sociological individualization theory[14] can have a positive or negative effect. You can do your own thing and build on the experience that hard work and audacity pay off, or in the eyes of your friends and acquaintances you can be the loser who has failed to live up to his own standards, or the unfortunate who couldn't strike the right balance between family and career. Today, even a medical license or an oh-so-respectable PhD can't prevent you from slipping into a difficult situation and losing your connection in a world that defines value on the basis of education, income, and profession. There are more and more "educational losers" from educationally strong backgrounds and professional write-offs from upwardly mobile families. When you run into them 20 years later, you find that the golden boy you knew in college and the woman you adored as an intern have become a cynical drinker and an exhausted single mother. Stories like these haven't been plucked from thin air. They are part of the atmosphere of fear in the middle class, which spreads imperceptibly but indisputably, like a soft rustling.[15]

But isn't this fear based on the false expectation of clear and continuous prosperity and respectability in middle-class society? Where is it written that the same conditions must produce the same results? Which member of the middle class really has to worry about being sucked into a spiral of poverty and landing in social oblivion? In a meritocratic society, the flip side of social advancement is social decline. Personal characteristics that do not translate into social assets naturally tip the scales here – otherwise the competition for coveted positions would make no sense. If failure is impossible, then success is worth nothing. No one in the middle class would dispute this.

The reason for this fear is a loss of orientation. Despite ample cushioning and solid qualifications, individuals feel more defenseless and vulnerable these days because the organic connection between the striving for autonomy and the bond of community appears to have been broken. When train drivers demand salaries that are in line with those of aircraft captains instead of the conductors with whom they share a company culture, then the pursuit of individual advantage has triumphed over the collective obligation to cooperate. The age in which individual capability and communal bonds went together in the mentality of the middle class is apparently over. Of course, there have always been performance individualists who rail against unions and parties and think the state is in the hands of predatory politicians, but now anyone who supports a policy of redistribution or advocates a balance of interests seems nostalgic at best, and usually just naïve or pigheaded. This indicates that middle-class milieus are not just growing more differentiated, they are actually growing apart. Because there is more for individual groups to acquire but less to distribute overall, these groups are working against each other more than with one another as they strive to advance. Petit bourgeois traditionalists, competent employees, the modern bourgeoisie, creative individualists, dynamic migration winners, and conservative members of the educated middle class hardly seem to have anything to say to one another anymore. They eyeball each other skeptically and enviously, but they don't feel comfortable in their own skins either. The fronts switch quickly and coalitions change with the wind – and in each case, the changes involve educational differences, generational differences, regional demarcations, shifts in industrial hierarchies, divergences in age brackets, relations within communities of descent, and the transformation of gender characters. And the questions are always the same: who feels cheated, who feels desired, who is expected to make sacrifices, who expects support, who stands at the front, and who makes up the rearguard of hoped-for, feared, unforeseen, and unpredictable social developments? There is no tacit guiding principle which, in view of an uncertain future, could have a mediating, bridging, or balancing effect between the different socio-moral milieus of the middle class.[16]

The only thing shared by these middle-class milieus, which both relate to and oppose one another, is a creeping sense of threat to the social status they have inherited, achieved, or asserted. Those who consider themselves middle class today don't believe the middle is shrinking when they look around at their friends, acquaintances, neighbors, and colleagues – but they also don't think that it's still growing. Even people of Turkish, Vietnamese, or Indian descent who have gained a foothold in the middle class of their adopted countries as entrepreneurs, doctors, and engineers can see that the middle class is growing more in their countries of origin, which is why even those who were born and raised outside of these countries can never entirely rule out the idea of returning.

In general, one gets the impression that the global middle class – thanks primarily to the economic dynamics, hunger for advancement, and demographic reserves in newly industrialized countries such as Brazil, India, China, and South Africa – is conquering the world as an engine for boosting economic productivity, expanding the entitlements of the welfare state, and developing a socio-moral sensitivity. Taking an annual income of between 30,000 and 60,000 dollars as their basis, banks such as Goldman Sachs estimate that there will soon be more people at these middle-income levels living in Asia and Latin America than in the G7 countries of the USA, Japan, Germany, the UK, France, Canada, and Italy.

The middle class is growing worldwide by around 80 million people every year, meaning that it will account for 50 percent of the global population by 2030, up from 29 percent today. Taking demographic change into account, 18 percent of the people in China will then belong to this category (up from 4 percent today), while only two percent of the people in Germany will (down from 6 percent today).[17]

While the middle class is exploding elsewhere, the postwar development of a leveled-out middle-class society has apparently reached its peak in Europe and Germany. In light of this, the middle class here can no longer count on expansion; it has to prepare itself for consolidation instead. It's true that foreign trade is growing year by year, German expertise is highly valued and in high demand especially in emerging countries, and Germany emerged from the 2008 crisis with perhaps the strongest national economy in the entire OECD world – but we have to acknowledge that we can't pin our hopes on this forever. The defensive, reserved, and pragmatic attitude of the German middle classes fits with the realization that the global situation is characterized by a constellation with new focal points and different dependencies. Social inequality has become a pervasive topic, not least because what's at stake is who is out in front, who is falling behind, and which *éminence grise* will be able to use their seasoned ability and superior knowledge to keep the peace.

This is the problematic issue of fear in today's middle-class society. People see themselves exposed to an open global situation in which a country's path-dependent experiences must confront the "best practices" that are in competition worldwide. It is a feeling of profound decentering that is creeping over and bearing down on all middle-class milieus.

Education is the signal issue relating to this fear.[18] It affects the many middle-class families which, despite the considerable efforts undertaken by the German education system after the "PISA shock[19]" at the start of the century, still believe their children are not in good hands in the public education system. Even the introduction of compulsory quality standards, experimentation with mixed year groups and cooperative learning projects, and more flexible learning times leading up to final exams cannot convince these parents that they should just send their children to the nearest local primary or secondary school, as their own parents did. Schools that emphasize social interaction to meet expanded inclusion criteria might lack support for math; schools that focus on teaching math and science might neglect the musical side of the educational process; and schools that teach bilingually right from the start might fall short when it comes to conveying values. In the wake of international comparative studies such as PISA, TIMUSS, and IGLU, which scrutinized the pedagogical performance and social permeability of the education systems in the OECD countries, a language of competencies has emerged which dictates what is most important: where will my child be primed – cognitively and communicatively, mentally and motivationally, emotionally and expressively – for an uncertain future in a confusing world?

The well-informed middle-class parents with higher education degrees who only want the best for their children are driving themselves crazy. And the education experts, learning coaches, and talk therapists they consult can only come up with conflicting advice that helps no one: you should trust in the developmental abilities of your own children, but not in the teaching abilities of normal schools. Critically minded parents who are dependent on encouragement and support when it comes to choosing the right kindergarten, the right elementary school, the right secondary school, and the right university therefore feel that they are on their own. They don't want to seem racist or elitist, but if they think their children are being used as a form of social cement and motivational filling for the children of parents who apparently have little inclination to advocate for the education and advancement of their own offspring, they will quickly fly into a fury about the presumed knowledge of educational administrators and school authorities.

Those who benefited from the expansion of education in the 1980s and 1990s are particularly susceptible to thinking that what they have achieved as families and attained as individuals could be threatened by outpaced migration losers and underprivileged people with little motivation. If a growing number of children all over Europe come from families with a migration background, the important aspect mustn't be where the parents of your children's classmates were born, but rather whether their forms of interaction, ideas about education, and sense of values are compatible with your own. Perfectly normal middle-class parents – whether they have a migration background or not – will flee from schools which seem to have a majority of children from homes that do not place the same value on education. By moving house or opting for a private school, they take refuge in educational environments where they believe they are among like-minded others. There is a socio-moral fear of contagion lurking under the surface here which means that, in the field of education in particular, segregation by immigrant group is increasingly being replaced with segregation by status group. In other words, the daughter of an engineer and a dentist from Afghanistan will raise no questions about social fit in school, while the son of a deliveryman and a geriatric nurse from Kosovo or Syria will only be welcomed with the same open-heartedness if he proves to be much smarter, nicer, and more charming than originally expected. This difference in attitude is what determines the difference in ranking.

The issue of education makes it clear that status fears are, first and foremost, fears about the future. Speculation about what is to come casts a pall of threat over all that one has achieved and wants to pass on. This applies especially to social positions that owe their respectability to the intangible value of knowledge and the symbolic commodities of meaning.[20] These include professions relating to corporate services such as organization, consulting, justification, and calculation; professions involving the production of value-added meaning such as design, communication, marketing, and advertising; professions offering practical life assistance such as doctor, lawyer, therapist, coach, and mediator; research and development professions such as engineering, mathematics, software development, and logistics; and, finally, professions in systems and social analysis such as analyst, behavioral researcher, demographer, cognitive psychologist, and opinion pollster.

All of these deal with concepts, advice, representations, algorithms, data, and visions that are worth their weight in gold today but could be junk tomorrow. In the early 1950s, the American sociologist C. Wright Mills published a book about white-collar workers which revealed that the new middle class of contemporary society is made up of people whose job is to apply knowledge and produce meaning.[21] They therefore make a living and justify their status with privileged access to a source of value based on the cycle of utilization through devaluation. What we refer to as innovation is nothing more than a different way of using things that already exist. Thanks to the web, people can suddenly earn a lot of money with things that were once free, such as communication, while search engines have made things that were once considered valuable, such as encyclopedias, totally worthless in one fell swoop. Who still remembers Kodak or Nokia? Who will remember Dell or Apple?

Mills highlighted the paradox of privilege and vulnerability that is characteristic of this new symbol-analytical and psycho-social middle class, and from this he identified the hidden status panic of its members. No one knows how long the kind of life guaranteed by a comfortable income and elevated esteem can be sustained. It is maddening, therefore, when the propagation of culture, knowledge, and meaning becomes open to negotiation – even in educational institutions – on account of a group viewed as a minority which has become uncoupled from the mainstream for a wide variety of reasons. What can one pass on to future generations if this is no longer assured? This manifest educational panic is the expression of a latent status panic.

Everyday battles on the lower rungs

Is this whole to-do about middle-class fear just an expression of cowardice, mawkishness, and despondency? Looking at sociological concepts such as the security paradox, which says that as security increases so does one's sensitivity to insecurity,[1] or the ceiling effect, which refers to the idea that the upper limit of a development has been reached, or the narcissism of minor differences, whereby small differences between people become the basis for big distances between them,[2] then we must conclude that social fears are concomitants of social positions entailing extensive demands for welfare and a high need for security. The better you are doing – but also the more unlikely it is that your standard of living will rise further, and the more similarity there is between different life situations – the more you will fear loss, curtailment, and neglect.

But what about the people in our society to whom this does not apply? What is feared by those who would even have to ring the doorbell to heaven? What do the fears of the lower class look like?

Low earners in Germany are rarely employed in industry these days; instead, most of them are service workers.[3] Around 15 percent of these people work as commercial cleaners, deliverymen, and carers, or for security companies, restaurants, salons, and discount stores.[4] These are routine service jobs that are poorly paid but demand a lot. If you cover a route for a private delivery company, you are your own logistics specialist, driver, hauler, and customer manager. Your vehicle has to be empty by the end of the day, regardless of how many stairs you had to climb, how high your customer contact rate was, or how heavy the packages were.[5] As a cleaner you have to keep up with the rest of your crew, even if you're only allotted six minutes to clean an office, including wiping down windowsills, emptying trash cans, and mopping. And as a carer you often have to tend to dying people for whom a friendly greeting or gentle hand on the forehead can change their whole day, even though your job is mostly about lifting and settling them.

All of this usually barely keeps the workers above the poverty line. At these income levels, the only way to feed a family or maintain the gap between benefits and wages for minimum income protection is through reinforcements based on a new regime of the welfare state. The principle that one should work hard during the week in order to be able to spend on the weekend or later in life does not apply in these cases. It applied to the dirty jobs in industry, but it is no longer true of the stressful jobs in the service sector. Workers can get by with routine service jobs, but not to the extent that they can compensate for the toil in their free time.

These are growth industries because households are

ordering more and more products online, there are more and more offices for knowledge workers and service providers, because vacations in one's own country are becoming more attractive especially in the high-price segment, and because the proportion of elderly people in the population continues to grow. Consequently, there is a lot of money to be earned with routine services. But the work done by hand here can't be taken over by the grippers of a robot. When it comes to routine services in particular, there are natural limits to the potential increase in profit through technical rationalization, not least because a smile or a humorous remark in passing is often what's required here. As far back as the late 1960s, the American economist William J. Baumol coined the idea of an endemic cost disease in the service industry to describe this state of affairs.[6]

Employers therefore can't earn more by using machines, only by putting pressure on people. In the routine services segment, this pressure is brought to bear from above by the bosses who dictate the pace, from below by the younger, fitter employees who get up the stairs more quickly, have more stamina, and don't yet have a family to feed, and from the side by co-workers who continually vie with each other for relief benefits and a better image. Routine service workers are hounded by this pressure every single day. They may feel armed against it when they are young and strong, but they come to fear it as they grow older and weaker.

This generally happens quite quickly. The body usually can't withstand the work of delivering, cleaning, nursing, serving, or selling for more than ten years. After that, you're consigned to the shelf and have to find some other way to get by. It's also important to know that the new "service proletariat," as opposed to the old "industrial proletariat," tends to be female and more ethnically heterogeneous, with more diffuse qualifications. Cleaning crews, nursing teams, and service staff are usually made up of women from all corners of the globe with a variety of formal qualifications – as senior administrative assistants, teachers, or trained translators, for example – many of which have not been recognized in their arrival country. In Europe, they are frequently circular migrants who spend most of their time in their destination country but still consider themselves to be Moldovans, Bulgarians, or Ukrainians. But most of them are actually the domestic-born descendants of the industrial working class.

In security, transportation, and industrial cleaning we find men over 40 who were once employed in manufacturing or construction, as well as young men with and without migration backgrounds who, on account of poor or non-existent educational qualifications, are forced to rely on the "everyman" labor markets for routine services.[7]

Pressure and fear are felt in the bodies of these men and women alike. After a statutory pay increase, cleaning firms will often simply cut the prescribed working time for a certain cleaning quota. Considering the very low degree of union organization in the routine services sector,[8] workers have to be able to personally put up a fight. But the more exhausted and depleted you feel, the harder this is. Out of a fear of being disparaged and weeded out, you simply accept the extra, virtually unpaid work forced on you by the new cleaning rosters.

Facility managers and overseers pass on the orders from above relatively coolly. There is an unspoken understanding that their implementation will come down to the cleverness of the individual. In commercial cleaning, the salient point is the distinction between cleaning visible surfaces, thorough cleaning, and cleaning only what is necessary. What will be visibly clean, how thorough must a thorough cleaning be, and when does cleaning need to be carried out at all? Trickery and deception is required if you're going to get anywhere. But if a customer complains, you'll quickly find yourself on the hit list. Then the deciding factor is not so much the shoddy work itself – because everyone knows shoddy work is part and parcel of the job – but the way in which the responsible person responds to the complaint of negligence. Do you have the strength to resist, do you let your supervisor tell you off, or do you just pack it all in? In any event, the confrontation immediately taxes the person as the whole – their physical constitution and their mental responsiveness. This is where we see the differences between the quick and clever or the alert and hard-nosed, but also between the cautious and skittish or the exhausted and wounded. Your willingness to fight for better or worse ultimately determines whether you will hold on to your job or be fired.

The fears in this new proletariat of routine services revolve around whether you can assert yourself against middle managers, young whippersnappers, and old hands; whether you'll be able to duck away and take a break; what kind of severance package you'll receive when you're booted out in middle age; and how you will cope with your fatigue.

This is really no different for the deliveryman than it is for the discount store clerk, or for the hairdresser than it is for the security guard, even though they themselves have their own ideas about who is in the better situation. In general, these jobs provide little opportunity for product pride or performance satisfaction. The customers usually remain anonymous, and the services leave no trace. Only nursing promises a chance to take personal satisfaction in providing care to someone else. However, interpersonal dependency generates different types of stress, which fundamentally demand the kind of professional distance expected of doctors and lawyers. What comes into play here is the fear of being unable to distance oneself enough, of being drained, or of becoming a "brute" as measured against one's own ethos.

All of these activities, which secure the framework for a high-productivity economy, push workers to the edge of exhaustion day after day, because putting pressure on people is the only way to rationalize and intensify their work performance. The fight for recognition that forms the backdrop to this thus takes on the archaic character of a fight between guard dogs in the service of lords and workers in the position of servants. As forms of personal domination have returned in the world of routine services, fear has become a prerequisite and condition for everyday survival. Fear guides the self-assertion practices of a directly and blatantly exploited human labor force in which, due to immigration or poor qualifications, very few people have any other choice.

Only occasionally does the anger erupt. Then the boss's coffee cup will be cleaned with the rag used to wash the floor, a pastry will be spat upon before the romantic breakfast is served, a mail bag will be thrown in the river, or an employee will just skip work altogether. You can breathe freely in that moment of anger, but it's of no use to the rest of your life.

The fragile self

Fear is exhausting. At its core, fear is a reaction to a perceived danger. It triggers a flight reflex in response to the expected harm to one's self or the reduction of one's possibilities. This saps energy, because a decision has to be made between fleeing or standing firm.

You break into a sweat when you think a stranger is at the door, when you're called in to your supervisor for some wrongdoing, or when you wake up in the middle of the night and realize you don't know what you want from your life. The fear of the void, which seems to come from nowhere, is part of the existential ambivalence of the other-directed character, who gears himself toward the expectations of others while simultaneously fearing their demands. The difficulty lies in saying "no," because this implies a "yes" to what you want for yourself and what you are willing to do. But how are you supposed to know what you want and what's important to you? In case of doubt, ensuring flexible adaptation is more important to the communicative and cooperative self of today than a fixation on self-imposed goals and plans. But the flip side of the fear of affronting someone and missing out on something is the fear of missing out on oneself.

Psychotherapy researchers have reported a shift in the clinical picture of psychological disorders – from neurotic conflicts to depressive states.[1] The typical problems of the present day are characterized not by the self whose desires bump up against the limits of what is permitted and who thus slips into a state of fearful expectation, but by the self who feels overwhelmed by many conflicting demands and expectations, finds it endlessly difficult to set limits, and is dominated by nagging doubts about the ability to sustain a relationship, feel pleasure, fall in love, or live life at all.

A number of studies have been dedicated to the psychological effects of the spread of the other-directed character in societies such as ours.[2] All of them describe the change in the individual, from a focus on conquest to a focus on empathy, as a shift in an existential question – namely, from "what am I allowed to do?" to "what am I capable of doing?"[3] The self that wants to subjugate the world is blocked at every corner by the "vexatious fact of society,"[4] with its solidified role expectations, hypocritical values, and allegedly protective walls. The neurotic conflict revolves around the experience of restriction, prohibition, and inhibition.[5] The sensitive self, by contrast, which seeks feedback and acknowledgement from others as it strives for self-realization, moves within the "social construction of reality"[6] right from the start. This self takes it for granted that its concept of itself is shaped only through its interaction with others. However, my fellow humans not only support my self-image, they also threaten my possibilities. The associated feeling of depressive inadequacy is aptly described by metaphors such as being suffocated, entangled, and engulfed.

The pivot from the corset of permission to the mobilization of capability affects key concepts in communal life. In school, children are no longer supposed to be lumped together and judged on the basis of standardized grades; instead, the talents and preferences of each child are supposed to be encouraged so that children can take full possession of the possibilities available to them. However, a self that is socialized in this way can only be indebted to itself and its own possibilities, no longer to externally set standards. The "negative" concepts of suppression and prohibition are replaced by "positive" concepts of openness and development. Then the normative concept does not involve removing the barriers that prevent the self from unfolding, but rather fueling the obligation to achieve individuation.

In keeping with this, company assessment centers are interested in the potential of their future employees. The concept of personal potential, which is difficult to pin down, signifies that companies are no longer looking to buy in labor power for certain units of time but rather labor capacity for different projects. In regimes of "flexible specialization," which are geared toward individual production for special customer wishes, you don't want people who always await instruction and quit at 5 o'clock sharp; instead, you need engaged, autonomous employees who continue thinking about a project even after work has ended for the day and who can understand the special concerns of clients from all over the world.

In a factory without walls, the labor situation is continually redefined depending on the task at hand. This blurs the boundaries between industrial manufacturing, services, and development. Individual employees must be able to deal with customers, machines, co-workers, product models, and materials. Communication skills, cooperative spirit, and systemic understanding are key-words in sectors that focus on added value, where there is no room for a calculated presence, an instrumental attitude toward work, or a narrow focus on one's job description. In this case, it is no longer possible to distinguish work from interaction.

Most people in modern society feel this optimization pressure not only in their job but also in their family life, in their free time – in their lives as a whole, actually. Young, highly educated women trust that they will be able to reconcile a challenging career with a tightly knit family, and the men of today who deal competently with risk don't want to end up as lone wolves. No one wants to just live for work or work to live; instead, they want to put as much life into their work and as much work into their life as necessary. They're concerned about attachment, sex, their clothing, professional challenges, their erotic aura, and their physical constitution. Boundary dissolution, individuation, flexibility, and creativity are the words that describe a life of other-directed intensification, one in which elation can suddenly turn into a feeling of running idle. Family planning becomes a nightmare, your partnership is stress tested, you get through team meetings in a vegetative state, and when you present the results of your work you feel that familiar tightness in your chest.

The mobilization of your abilities – in every direction and on every level – runs aground on the abrupt question of what it is that you want. What's the point of it all? What does it all amount to? What do I want out of life? These are questions born of the fear for oneself, and they can be very exhausting.

You feel harassed, driven, and attacked. Everything seems dull, flat, and unappealing. You wake up in the morning and feel wiped out, as if you hadn't slept at all. The remainder of your self – the part that makes the coffee and turns on the computer – can't ward off the self-destructive inclination to question everything, brood incessantly about whether there is a way out, or lament how isolated you feel from what's happening at work or at home. Why does everything always go wrong, for heaven's sake?

Apparently the fear of not being able to do anything right can, at a certain point, turn into a fear of having done everything wrong. The mania for optimization merely covers up the existential anxiety. Setting priorities is good advice, but it overlooks the fact that one must first have a sense of these priorities. This may be especially true of the generation that comes from saturated conditions, and for whom the relationship between birthrate and job availability is very favorable – more favorable, in any case, than that of their parents' baby-boomer generation. This is "Generation Y," today's 25- to 35-year-olds, who are said to be pragmatic and sensitive, with an awareness of their own competence, but who are focused on attention, encouragement, and praise, and who lean toward materialistic security values and post-materialistic self-development values. These contradictory tendencies can, on the one hand, be interpreted as evidence of a world view shaped by self-assurance, soberness, and open-mindedness, or, on the other hand, as the expression of an attitude toward life which means they do not want to be deprived of anything and therefore try to reconcile everything.

The work/life balance issue is so critical to this young generation because it touches on gender relations, the idea of achievement, and the understanding of personal happiness. Young women no longer think about having to make a tragic choice between professional success and a happy family life, which means the division of gainful employment, childcare, emotional support, and housekeeping has to be negotiated between the sexes. The concept of achievement can therefore no longer be centered solely on one's career, for either men or women; instead, it encompasses everyday life as the basis of a mutually negotiated and agreed-upon existence. A certain degree of material security, a certain level of comfort, and a reasonably functioning public infrastructure are considered essential to this. But personal happiness is no longer measured solely in terms of professional progress or the classic status symbols of the leveled-out middle class. No one wants to spend their life waiting in line for the elevator to social advancement. Friendship is of primary importance, value is placed on a thriving living environment that is untroubled by unpleasant outsiders and free of environmental pollutants, and a challenging and satisfying professional life is considered vital.[7] Neither the internet nor the experience of global tourism have changed these positively idyllic notions in any way. Because there are no suitable templates or scripts for this desired way of living, however, life as a whole appears to be an achievement of the self, which cannot fall back on any primary or elementary sphere of achievement.

But the language of development, growth, and transformation, which is steeped in humanism, provides the formulas that highlight the open, all-encompassing, and multi-faceted process of living.[8] According to this, a failed life is not measured against a law that was defined from the start or a goal to be reached at the end, but instead against the potential abundance available to an individual in a given social situation and biographical moment. How this potential is realized in an individual's life is determined by the ways in which the individual renounces, rejects, neglects, or misses his or her opportunities.[9]

When opportunities are neglected or missed, the failure is immediately apparent. Missed opportunities are irrevocably lost. The self has failed to seize the moment and can only hope that a similar opportunity will arise again later. This applies not only to business life or the scramble for a better position, but also to the unfortunate words spoken in the morning or the unexpected tryst in the afternoon. The more someone is convinced of the success of their own life, the harder it is to accept a missed opportunity.

Neglected opportunities, on the other hand, may yet be recovered – upon payment of a late fee, of course. Neglect sometimes leads to a second chance. Often, however, things that were neglected in the past will weigh on you in the present. The self is then consumed by the notion that the neglected opportunity was not just one of many, but was actually the decisive opportunity in your life. You then focus all of your efforts and aspirations on making up for the opportunity neglected in the past – which can sometimes blind you to the new opportunities available in the present. The self blocks itself because it is mourning for what is long gone.

While missed and neglected opportunities are things that happen to you, renouncing and rejecting opportunities involves a certain level of decision making. When something is renounced, the self refrains from doing one thing, as hard as it may be, and does something else instead. This is usually a fairly mundane process. Over the course of time, you choose one option from a range of possibilities so that you can continue to act. When options are rejected, however, you cull the seemingly unattractive and unsuitable ones in order to better till your field of potential actions. Of course, there is no guarantee that renunciation or rejection was the right thing to do. In retrospect, it may turn out that you favored the wrong thing and shelved the right thing. Every important life decision is a gamble which, as Kierkegaard would put it, must be lived forwards and understood backwards. And this may be where the actual reason for a failed life lies: that the self wants to get around the risk of making a decision, of saying "yes" to this and "no" to that. Although hesitation and procrastination can be smart and human responses,[10] the fear of those who are undecided – who, like the 28-year-old protagonist of Benjamin Kunkel's novel,[11] are convinced that postponement is a substitute for immortality – is quite possibly the fear of our times. It defines a life spent in a waiting room, as you sit and watch the information board for the decisive call.

Rule by nobody

The expectation of deterioration, loss, or injury is frightening, but so is the perception of inundation, inflation, or the dissolution of boundaries. The fear that you're getting too little of what everyone desires as compared to your peer group is infuriating, and the fear that the sense of proportion for what is necessary and possible is getting lost is panic-inducing. The fear of curtailment and degradation for the individual is matched by the fear of the collapse and devaluation of the whole.

It is immediately apparent that social conditions can worsen intolerably when these two things collide: when the fear of maintaining one's own position in the system is accompanied by the fear that the entire system of justified positions will collapse. In sociological terms, we would say that a social system slips into a precarious situation when diverse experiences of a hitherto unknown disparity in the distribution of privileges and risks mix with a general sense of anomie regarding the benchmarks of performance effort and rewards for success.

We apparently have two things in overabundance

today: money at our disposal, and data on individual people. "Today" refers to the period after the global economic and financial crisis of 2008 and the associated sovereign debt crisis of 2011 (which affected more than just Europe) on the one hand, and, on the other, the period following the revelations about the espionage activities coordinated between systemically relevant search engines and secret state intelligence services and directed against countless internet users. In terms of the legitimation of both capitalism and the internet, nothing is now as it once was.

Even before June 5, 2013 – when Edward Snowden first informed the public, via the *Guardian*, of the extensive surveillance activities being carried out across the entire World Wide Web by the National Security Agency in the USA – the renowned American market research survey known as the Harris Poll determined that just 8 percent of the people questioned in 2012 considered social media companies such as Facebook, Twitter, and YouTube to be honest and trustworthy.[1] According to estimates by the United Nations, around 40 percent of the world's population now uses the internet, and more and more people are communicating via social networks – but only about 10 percent of them actually trust the companies that make this communication possible. These free services are ultimately not free, as any user who has searched online for routes through the Andes or winter tires for their SUV realizes when they find themselves confronted the next morning with digital ads from tour operators specializing in Nepal or watch brands offering big, expensive mechanical timepieces. How do they know that I am, in fact, interested in Tibet and have actually flirted with the idea of buying myself a high-price watch? Am I already in the cross-hairs of "emotional targeting" that has identified me as a priority consumer for a luxury goods company?

Since Edward Snowden's revelations at the latest, we know that not only is a tremendous amount of data being traded on and through the web, but that personal data which can be traced back through IP addresses is being passed on to national intelligence services, where it is collated, compared against other metadata about circles of contacts on the web, and analyzed for suspicious behavior. The NSA is considered to be a very generous employer for mathematicians, all of whom are occupied with decrypting potentially encrypted communication on the World Wide Web. But unlike the genius Alan Turing, who worked on behalf of His Majesty the King at Bletchley Park, 50 miles northwest of London, during World War II and was able to crack the supposedly unbreakable German Enigma encryption system, the race between encryption and decryption is no longer a competition between nations at war, but rather between the state that wants to make itself invulnerable and the vulnerable individuals who want to protect their personal and private information. The sense of unease triggered by unsolicited advertising has turned into the fear of a "Big Brother" who ceaselessly records everything I reveal about myself on portable computers. Can I continue to communicate and express myself in emails and chat rooms, or through WhatsApp and Xing, without having to fear a knock on my door in the night?[2]

One may presume, however, that certain commercial search engines now know far more about us than any national intelligence services, whether they operate from the USA or the UK. Google is the role model for the NSA. The mission to know everything can only be fulfilled by a machine that permanently learns how to know everything.

Google naturally doesn't force anyone to do anything, but as soon as we take advantage of a digital amenity while jogging (measuring our running speed or calorie consumption), taking pictures (adjusting objects or modulating colors), driving (optimizing fuel consumption or reporting wear and tear), looking up travel information, banking online, or searching for a museum's opening hours, when using Twitter, email, or text messages, when ordering things online, consulting Wikipedia, or looking up the origin of a well-known saying – then Google is there. Google generates logs of web access, sensor frequencies, and information sharing which are automatically stored in databases, organized, and made accessible to others. This gives rise to large volumes of data from diverse sources, from which special data sets can be derived based on different parameters, which are then peddled in data markets. A (naturally commercially motivated) browser which is required for viewing sites on the World Wide Web is already advertising a service for watching the watchmen: "See who's watching you on the internet. Shine a light on the third-party websites that are collecting data about your online activities."[3]

If this data can be traced back to me, then I can be addressed as an individual example of a particular type, with characteristic movement profiles, consumer preferences, judgments of taste, dependency tendencies, and rejection affects. The mathematics of Google – with the help of cognitive psychology, decision theory, framing concepts, and emotional grids – can tailor big data to the needs of various customers: companies wanting to advertise their expensive durables or cheap consumables to specific target groups, entertainment industries wanting to supply children with animated games and adults with ritual ones, health insurers searching for criteria for staggered rates and starting points for preventive programs, neuroscientists wanting to develop neurotechnical implants or neuromorphic computers, and, indeed, intelligence services wanting to identify suspicious impulses and thoughts among particular groups and individuals in the population.

What's frightening about this is not so much that new volumes of data are being generated day after day, but that we now have the computing capacity to store this data apparently forever and continually serve it up for new purposes. Waste information no longer composts itself as it did in many of the totalitarian surveillance systems of the past;[4] it now remains available as informative material to be found by future generations of clever seekers and searchers. The fact that something I post online in a fit of madness or desire is technically unforgettable in the global cloud can, to borrow Heidegger's words, fill the individual *Dasein*, or existence – which anticipates its own death from the very start – with dread. The thought that nothing fades away in a web ruled by Google is catastrophic. For historical beings, memory is based on forgetting. Those who can't leave anything behind will never get anywhere. Cognitive psychology has taught us that learning is based on unlearning, so we only get smarter when we can let things rest.

But we don't seem to have a choice. After all, we willingly supply the data that threatens to dominate us in the form of algorithms for various types of "targeting." As soon as we carry an iPad around with us, use a GPS device on our morning run in an unfamiliar city, or connect to a digital cable television, we are caught in the trap. We don't have to do any of this, of course, but the price of refusal is fairly high. Gilles Deleuze foresaw the approach of these "forms of ceaseless control in open sites"[5] as early as 1990. This thinker, who described the "thousand plateaus" of our society,[6] was interested in understanding the relationship between the apparent openness of our technological infrastructure and the heightened control in our personal and private lives. Deleuze would see the web as the epitome of a control society which functions not by means of internment and closure, as the classic disciplinary society would, but by means of ceaseless openness and instant communication. Everything is communication, and no one can escape it. "One cannot not communicate," as Paul Watzlawick famously said in a dictum that effectively checkmates the individual.[7] So the search for universals of communication, as Deleuze put it, which lies at the core of Google's mathematics should strike fear into our hearts.

This is the thinking behind the criticism of "Silicon Valley capitalism," which aims to leave us no breathing space as it transforms every aspect of everyday life into productive, symbolic, social, or economic capital. Hidden within this criticism is a fear of drowning in the whirlpool of all-round development and increased potentiation. What can we do to defend our private sphere, and how can we extricate ourselves from the communication networks we've joined? Isn't striking against the network like striking against oneself?[8]

This fear is now making it possible for a hatred of the system to be expressed by generations who imagined themselves to be beyond fear and hatred. "Why we are allowed to hate Silicon Valley" is the title of an article which claims, with an air of logical despair, that the "invisible barbed wire" of the digital control society is not even apparent to those who erected it. Instead, users are told that they can gain clarity by using the right tools. "This is where the 'digital debate' leads us astray: it knows how to talk about tools but is barely capable of talking about social, political, and economic systems that these tools enable and disable, amplify and pacify. When these systems are once again brought to the fore of our analysis, the 'digital' aspect of such tool-talk becomes extremely boring, for it explains nothing."[9]

Another latent and lasting fear is spreading with the proliferation of something else: money. The amount of money in circulation and what this expresses is beyond our normal economic comprehension. First we were told that the inconceivable amount of money stashed away in bad loans is what led us into the financial crisis, and now we're supposed to believe that the inconceivable amount of money provided by the central banks will lead us out of it.

According to the American economist Richard Duncan, the amount of money all around the globe was 2,000 percent higher in 2000 than it had been 30 years before,[10] when the world was still divided in two and the USA was the undisputed leading power in the West. The amount of money in the USA alone – including cash and credit balances as well as credit-like financial investments, and adjusted for purchasing power – rose from 315 billion to around 2 trillion dollars in the last third of the twentieth century.[11] But this is not even covered by the economic performance that is usually represented by a country's GDP. Overall in the OECD countries, the ratio of available money to GDP increased from 68 percent in 1970 to 109 percent in 2006. In other words, the continual growth of goods and services cannot keep up with the explosive growth in the amount of money in circulation. Anyone hoping for social relations to prosper will naturally wonder why the production of physical goods and tangible services has drifted apart from the pure generation of money – and how long this can carry on.

It may be that the monetary collapse of 2008, which was ultimately triggered by the insolvency of an investment bank, was actually necessary. When Lehman Brothers went bankrupt, an entire system of money management and money creation was called into question all at once. In banks all over the world, huge sums suddenly appeared which were covered by literally nothing at all. In the space of just a few days in September 2008, another inconceivable sum of money was "burned" in the global financial markets. The estimates range from two to seven trillion dollars.[12]

The looming implosion of the entire internationally networked money supply necessitated the immediate intervention of governments whose officials wanted to prevent a repeat of the Great Depression in the late 1920s and its infamous social consequences. We may recall how the concerted action of the central banks led to an unprecedented level of intervention in financial markets that had become incapable of self-regulation. Barack Obama had been elected as the new US President but had not yet been sworn in. On Monday, September 15, 2008,

Lehman Brothers declared bankruptcy; on the following Tuesday, American International Group (AIG) – the second-largest insurance company in the world – was bailed out, followed by the investment bank Merrill Lynch and the huge Washington Mutual savings bank. The United States Federal Reserve under chairman Ben Bernanke, who had made a name for himself as a professor of economics at Princeton University with his studies of the global economic crisis of the 1930s, bought massive amounts of treasury bonds and mortgage-backed securities, as it was said, and, in doing so, indirectly printed money on yet another incomprehensible scale. The Fed's total assets have risen from 869 billion dollars on August 1, 2007 to, most recently (i.e., the start of 2017), 4.45 trillion dollars. The Federal Reserve thus became the most important financer in the financial market. The final state of this targeted intervention program was known as "quantitative easing," which saw the Fed buying treasury bonds and mortgage-backed securities for 85 billion dollars every month to bring down long-term interest rates. This measure was gradually rolled back starting in December 2013 to decrease the money supply again and slowly accommodate the markets to more realistic interest rates. This has naturally affected international financial flows which, to the dismay of emerging economies, follow the monetary policy of what is still the most important reserve currency in the world.

Every country around the world now has "systemically important banks" that would have to be bailed out with a great deal of money if they were at risk of failing, as well as a "market-compliant democracy" for which the respective governments must demand the fealty of their citizens. The European Central Bank (ECB) went so far as to bail out not only individual banks, but entire countries that had gotten themselves deeply into debt with cheap euros. If necessary, the ECB would buy up unlimited government securities from countries in the euro group that found themselves unable to refinance on the financial markets at tolerable interest rates. "Whatever it takes" was the promise made by Mario Draghi at an investment conference in London on July 16, 2012, making the announcement that the financial market players had apparently been waiting for. "And believe me, it will be enough," the President of the European Central Bank had added. Taking a step back, this strategy might appear strange. Can limitation through the abolition of limits work in the long term?

This whole recent episode, which was so outstandingly important in terms of financial policy and monetary history, and which has continued in the form of a European sovereign debt crisis that is far from over, raises the worrying question of what the public can still believe these days when it comes to money. What does money represent? Who vouches for its value? How is it created? What is its function? These are questions born of the fear that the monetary and financial economy represents a perhaps necessary but certainly not sustainable system of spreading risk and shifting repayment.

The idea propounded by Aristotle and still shared in principle by orthodox economists – namely, that money facilitates exchange and stores value – would seem to be common sense.[13] Money transcends the simple exchange of goods by mediating it in the form of abstract, countable, and accountable units, and it represents the industriousness of its owner, who can use it to buy anything that can be sold. Money helps trade flourish, and money motivates the players in an economy.

But what's the point of a boundless proliferation of money that has been divorced from the trade in goods and services, and what kind of industriousness is behind the tremendous capital gains of monetary asset holders in an age of deregulated money markets? For the people who work hard and follow the rules, capitalism today seems like nothing more than a money machine that makes the rich even richer and the poor even poorer. The capital market presents itself as an intrinsically dynamic system that is controlled largely by computers and is connected worldwide, whose only law is to turn invested money into even more money. Mediation through goods that must be manufactured, sold, and consumed seems to be of secondary importance. The primary focus is on balance sheet listings that mysteriously transform minuses into pluses and pluses into minuses. To this end, figures are put into circulation, bets are placed, and transactions are conducted that promise the players fantastic opportunities which are, of course, tied to invisible risks.

It is apparent that not all of the money being used here has been earned elsewhere through the production and sale of goods and services; instead, by means of certain financial instruments that produce and sell debt, money is literally being created out of nothing. And the more money that is created, the greater the pressure exerted by the unused monies and excess reserves in the portfolios that are established to balance the risks. These are then transformed into debts that can be traded by clever financial market players for their own account or that of a third party, so there is no end to the endogenous creation of money.

The central bank of the state comes into play as a lender of last resort if it looks like the pyramid scheme is about to be busted and capital investment values are at risk of general collapse. But the process continues as long as everyone involved believes in what they are doing – until a failure at a single point triggers a chain reaction of failures, and all of the contingency insurance that was meant to be a reserve for the repayment promises that were stacked on top of one another is revealed to be nothing but a lie. Up to that point, the colorful characters who tell great stories to explain their opaque certificates will rake in high bonuses and amass extraordinary incomes. In any case, the rhetoric of conviction has little to do with the validity of mathematical calculations. But fraud is often a retrospective offense, not something that is always intended from the outset.

For the 99 percent of people who find out about this "intrinsic behavior" of monetary increase through the mass media, the only problem is that the demonization of greed and the revolutionary and restorative demand for a "reversal of the starting point"[14] (according to which the economy must serve the people again instead of the people serving the economy) both overlook the systemic nature of the capitalist monetary economy.

Anyone who invests their savings in a fund at the recommendation of a friendly financial advisor, or takes out a private pension to close a gap in coverage, or buys a sizeable car on installments, is participating in a system that consists of relationships between creditors and debtors. This even applies to a simple savings account. As soon as you take the cash you were fortunate enough to inherit and deposit it note for note in the bank, your money is gone. Banks famously do not stockpile the money of their private customers; they put it to work by entrusting it to a creditworthy debtor who promises to pay it back with added interest. And all you are left with is a figure printed on a receipt which says that, somewhere in the world, natural or legal persons exist who have promised to give your money back to you with an interesting premium.

If a senior executive finds himself unable to service the loan for his house after being laid off, or a country can no longer service its loans in the international financial markets on account of an abrupt rise in interest rates, it is not a serious problem as long as the impending credit defaults have been securitized and insured. But if there is a sudden agglomeration of such defaults, then even the best securitizations of loan portfolios by the relevant agencies will be of no use – because the holders of credit default swaps are themselves indebted to creditors who have placed their trust in a promise of repayment based on mathematical calculations. A "black swan" that is identified as such by an observer in the system, who then places a speculative bet on this discovery, can cause the entire system to collapse. "If a financial crisis is triggered by a particular event or failure of policy," declared a recently rediscovered theorist of the fundamental financial instability of the capitalist economy,[15] "the overall financial structure must be such that individual failure can trigger a chain reaction of failures."

Consequently, it is not enough to define money as a medium of exchange or value storage in a financial system designed for self-exploitation. Money is an expression of a relationship between a creditor and a debtor which is based on nothing more than a prom-ise.[16] As long as the market participants – all of us – place their trust in this promise, everything will be alright. The process of financialization can, in principle, go on forever. But as soon as someone in the crowd shouts that the emperor has no clothes, an abyss opens up, and it becomes apparent that all of the promises were deceitful and no debtor can be trusted anymore. In a single blow, a system of trust then turns into a system of fear.

The fear triggered by the masses of data that can be retrieved from anywhere, and the masses of money being created incessantly by players in the financial mar-kets, is a fear of being entangled in a system that one has created oneself. Every time I access the internet, I make myself vulnerable, and every time I deposit money into my account, I enter into a financial relationship based on reciprocal receivables which want to use money to make more money. We've been told that we're always being watched on the World Wide Web, but we still write that next email; we've seen speculative bubbles grow, stock market crises erupt, and monetary transac-tions come to a halt, but when it comes to the interest on our larger or smaller investments, we're immedi-ately prepared to ride the roller coaster all over again. Apparently no boundaries can be set, and apparently no one is responsible for it.

The fear of a world on the brink can be mitigated by accusing others and protesting against the system, but it cannot be eliminated altogether. This is because it is not the fear of the "big, bad other" that deceives, compels, and dominates us. It is the fear of our own pos-sibilities, to which we allow ourselves to be misled and seduced. Spirals of entanglement, feedback loops, and confidence multipliers bind individuals to a system that evades all control and ultimately destroys itself through strange irregularities. The fear that proliferates following functional and legitimacy crises of capitalism and the internet is the fear of self-regulatory systems that are governed by the reactions, choices, and decisions of the individuals involved – and not by methods of incorporation, but by methods of incitement and transgression. It is the fear that no one is in control of this process because everyone is involved in it and everyone expects to get something out of it. The fear of an excess that surpasses all measure is the fear of the rule by nobody[17] in which everybody plays a part.

The power of emotion

What can we do with the realization that we ourselves are creating the fear we experience in the face of a threatening world? This feeling of threat and concern can't be explained or argued away. After all, the fear of not being able to maintain one's social status through the generations, or the fear of another financial collapse that would take personal savings and private pensions down with it, cannot be dismissed out of hand. We can see that fears are dependent on our demands, but reducing our demands does not necessarily reduce our fear. We have to be able to generally rely on something, even if deep down we know that everything in life just keeps moving along.

The communication of fear is subject to a strange inconsistency in modern society. As individuals, we don't want to seem fearful especially to our friends and acquaintances. It is not particularly attractive to express feelings of helplessness, deadlock, or paralysis. The fearful self is not an individuality pattern[1] that scores points with others. The ideal of coolness that is so prized today in pop culture practically polices itself by censoring the expression of fear. On the other hand, the expression of fear in public can always claim to have something authentic about it. A confession of fear is indisputable because no one can object to the appropriateness of the declaration, only to the credibility of the speaker. Anyone who uses fear as a justification for their opposition to something is legitimized – particularly when they do so in the name of others who dare not do it, who have no voice, or who haven't yet grasped the situation. Fear expressed by proxy can pose serious difficulties for the leadership of a country, a company, or a civic organization.

In other words: announcing your fear can make you appear weak in private and strong in public. But the temptation is always there to deceive yourself and others. You'd rather not reveal to your partner that you lie awake at night brooding about a treacherous comment made by your boss, or that you're forever thinking about your changing sexual appetites. Even to friends, you'll only make a few passing melancholy remarks in a humorous tone. Your fear is stuck in an endless loop of dark thoughts that can't find the right way to express the feeling of suffocation.

The public incitement of fear, on the other hand, follows certain templates that illustrate worst-case scenarios. We are usually told we face the threat of environmental or economic apocalypse, which leaves us very little time to make radical changes. And the reference object for this fear is correspondingly vague: you may fear for your children's future or for the survival of our blue planet. Anyone who argues that pensions are actually relatively safe thanks to the pay-as-you-go system, or that in the old industrialized countries in particular, which still indulge in the ideology of growth, the air is getting better and the rivers cleaner comes across as either an absurd skeptic or a cold cynic. The fear put forth as an argument in public debates eludes the principle of argumentation.[2]

The paradox of communicating fear[3] is that the authenticity of the expression is often purchased at the price of the remoteness of the reasoning. What could the inevitable collapse of the planet – under the rallying cry of "More money!" – have to do with my personal and private situation as a "precariously prosperous" middle-aged, middle-class citizen? In a nutshell: there is a danger that you are deluding yourself in your fear.

The underlying question here is whether fear can be communicated at all. After all, the experience of fear involves a sense of being alone with the feeling that everything is falling apart and nothing can hold together. For Kierkegaard, this was evidence of the modern phenomenon of discovering that we must live our lives ourselves and through ourselves. This fact is what drives the self – which can avail itself of nothing and no one – into the arms of fear. During the Great Depression in the late 1920s, Heidegger wrote that this *Dasein*, which must be itself, is suspended in nothingness.[4] This is the danger that promises salvation.

For Heidegger, fear is not necessarily a negative concept. As an affect of selfhood, it can actually be positive when the *Dasein*, in its "being-toward-death," dissociates itself from others and their idle chatter. Instead of talking in circles, one becomes aware of oneself. Heidegger's existential heroism views the fundamental loneliness of the self as the prerequisite for the inner collectedness of the self.[5]

It is always illuminating for a certain socio-historical moment when the silence surrounding fear is broken – when the fear that seems to be buried in the personal and private sphere is expressed in a way that is considered generally applicable to the public. The fearful self is invoked as the subject of fear and can consider its flaw to be a mark of distinction. Then we no longer need to explain our fears because they have already been understood. And then fear no longer separates individuals, it brings them together as a whole.

This is where the politics of fear come into play, which escalate personal experiences of degradation and group-specific fears of loss into a general expression of helplessness and threat. Expressions of dismay that speak to a "loss of utopia," a "regime of locusts," "buying time," or "the specter of capital" generate an atmosphere of social instability that holds out the prospect of predictable crises, systems susceptible to failure, and expanding social divisions. None of this is plucked from thin air, but it makes a big difference whether you believe you live in a failing, changing, or vanishing world.

What's important here is the instance in which emotions are consolidated. Long before the age of financialization, when Germany seemed to be endlessly waiting for social change in the 1980s, the economists Guy Kirsch and Klaus Mackscheidt developed a typology of affective political leadership.[6] They distinguished between demagogues, statesmen (or stateswomen, we should add), and ordinary officeholders. The typology works with classic motifs: the demagogue intensifies the people's fear and throws a scapegoat at their feet, who is blamed for all of their misery; the officeholder numbs the fear by painting a picture of social reality which lacks all unsettling and threatening aspects; and the statesman shows how the fear is founded in reality and how we can confront our fears nonetheless without condemning everything wholesale.

We immediately think of the populist instigators who warn against the extinction of a nation or against the euro debt pact; we hope instead for the great oratory of the statesman or stateswoman who acknowledges the limits and flaws of capitalism but also points out ways to evade the hazards; and, for the time being, we settle for the officeholder who competently and consistently solves the practical problems that arise day after day.

The most insightful aspect of Kirsch and Mackscheidt's book is its correction of a logical but misguided understanding of politics. We are quick to assume that the purpose of politics is to solve communal problems which, though they affect everyone, are beyond the problem-solving capacity of the individual. Whenever the call goes out in times of crisis for experts who know something about economics or management, we are falling back on this understanding of politics as an arena for negotiating strategies to solve collective problems. The fact that election campaigns are actually more about allegiance, devotion, anger, envy, ill will, and enthusiasm than about objectively analyzing various ideologically accented approaches to solving problems must seem like a regrettable side effect of rituals of mass mobilization. When politics gets people so riled up that their eyes blaze, then according to this understanding of politics, it no longer has anything to do with the necessary debate about the best way of supplying and distributing resources, but has instead degenerated into sentimentality and affective theatricality.

For Kirsch and Mackscheidt, this popular denunciation of the business of politics as a politics of illusion, which operates with emotions instead of arguments, is based on a halved concept of the political. The political dispute doesn't really revolve around whether the top tax rate should be 47.5 or 49.5 percent, whether extra retirement benefits should be paid to women who had children before 1992 or before 1989, or whether there should be a 0.05 percent or 0.03 percent tax on all financial transactions – it revolves around whether the tax rate should be raised appreciably for the rich and super-rich, whether mothers who put their careers on hold to raise their children because they had no access to a kindergarten or all-day school should have their parenting recognized in the form of a pension, or whether politicians are prepared to keep a check on risky spot trading in the financial market. This is not a debate about improving the supply of goods for citizens, it is a fight about granting social rights to groups and establishing social boundaries in general.

The interests of individuals do not play the main role in this dispute – ideas about our coexistence do. And these ideas are embodied in the political confrontation between politicians. This is why political struggle is always a struggle for identification.

Politics without passion, without emotional energy, without the dynamics of psyches encountering and repelling one another, and without fear and desire is no politics at all. In a representative democracy, political leaders are the projection anchor for these political affects. When viewed in this light, an election campaign, with its mixture of argumentative explication and personal confrontation, does not serve primarily to prepare a factually founded mandate between voters and the person they elect, but rather to lay the foundation for a personally mediated relationship of trust between citizens and their representatives – or to reveal the existence of a serious representation deficit.[7]

The problem of fear is implicit in the question of trust. The public looks at the men and women in the running and searches for signs of how they interpret the present social situation. Should we be afraid? Can we live with our fears? Do we dare hope for a world without the fear of fear? The demagogue says: "I'm one of you! I understand your situation and I empathize with you! And I'm telling you: we are being betrayed and sold out!" Demagogic discourse uses fear as the basis of a policy of social separation. It implies that there is a ruling class who is feathering its own nest and pushing large sections of society to the margins. These oppressed and marginalized forces are invoked as a testament to the disorder of society as a whole, and with their desires and drives, needs and goals, fantasies and visions, they represent everything that is ignored and opposed by prevailing opinion.

Demagoguery elevates fear to the measure of distinction between truth and lies. If you are afraid, you are in the right, because the prevailing chatter is designed solely to lead us to believe that the situation can be brought under control through endless discussion and compromise. Much like psychoanalysis, demagogic discourse constructs a sphere of latency which stands in opposition to the sphere of what is manifestly negotiated. The demagogue can therefore portray herself[8] as the representative of "senseless frustrations,"[9] someone who promises to relieve the fear that, in truth, affects everyone. She can express all of our concerns without inhibition or restriction – not because she is superior to us, but because she is so psychologically similar to us.

The ordinary officeholder, on the other hand, banks on the relative solidity of fear management in the ruling classes of society. Her political success is predicated on calmly pointing out that ruin can be averted by progressing and learning. She can avail herself of a reality of surprisingly reliable expectations even as central expectations collapse. While large sections of the public sit and wait for the masterstroke that is supposed to lead us out of the crisis, the officeholder has left all admonishers and laggards behind her long ago with her fast and flexible policy of small steps. The quiet force she embodies is based on a pragmatism that skirts the big questions and focuses instead on gradually working through the problems of the moment. Fear is not established in images of threat and endangerment, it is processed on sight, in a sense.

What distinguishes the officeholder is not her superior knowledge or exemplary behavior, but rather the "above-average averageness"[10] of her attitude toward life. There is nothing aristocratic or eccentric about it. Signs of fear do emerge in her self-presentation, but they appear alongside signs of joy, confidence, and weariness. She conveys to the public that she is in no way a special person with extraordinary gifts. The only resource of courage that sets her apart is the courage to wield power.

The ordinary officeholder might well cope very efficiently with the problems of political governance, but she also lulls her fearful constituents by disregarding all experiences and worries that could cause fear. This sustains an unspoken pact of fear between the officeholder and her followers, which sweeps aside ambiguities, feelings of vertigo, and the urge to flee. The officeholder gives citizens the sense of calm they need to hold onto their guiding principles in confusing situations; but she also does not make demands on them to ensure they don't lose courage in testing situations. In the end, the political success of the officeholder could have the same roots as her almost inevitable failure: blocking developmental processes, defending immovable borders when encountering the world, and maintaining rigid defense mechanisms.

The statesman is an exceptional figure who owes his existence to a fortunate coincidence of subjective disposition and objective opportunity. Winston Churchill would never have become Winston Churchill without World War II, Willy Brandt would not have been Willy Brandt without the leeway offered by "peaceful coexistence," and Nelson Mandela would not have been Nelson Mandela without the long wave of decolonialization. But without Churchill, World War II would have taken a different course, without Brandt there would have been no *Ostpolitik*, and without Mandela, South Africa would be a different place.

The statesman resonates with his electors not because he confirms the imperatives and prohibitions of their self-image, but because, on the contrary, he believes the boundaries that confine and define individuals can be overcome. His rhetoric is directed at the despondent *I* who is addressed as part of the *we*. And his message is "We will resist, even if it takes blood, sweat, and tears!"

or "We will not perish if we admit our guilt!" or "If you fall, you can stand up again!"

The statesman exemplifies an inner sovereignty that has been formed through opposition and defeat. This is the source of his counterpoint to doomsday sentiments, assumptions of inevitability, and blockade mentalities. The passion of resentment and temptations of dormancy are pitted against a belief in the openness of the future. Nothing has to stay the way it is; we can give something up in order to gain something else; we can become different by uniting with others and creating a new framework together.

The demand for self-transcendence is what causes the relationship between the statesman and the people to be characterized by tensions and contradictions. This relationship is not geared toward the preservation of what people already have or the disinhibition of their desires. Instead, it aims to expand and enrich the life possibilities and potential experiences of citizens in and through politics. As the one who opens the door and leads the way, the statesman takes on the spiritual role of presenting fear as something that can be controlled by loosening one's inner shackles and opening up social boundaries.

This is why rejection and affection, disparagement and gratitude toward the statesman are often so close together in the public's sentiments. While the ordinary officeholder can count on the unexcited support of wide swathes of the population whose fears she soothes, the statesman faces passionate opposition as well as passionate devotion.

His followers will praise his unfamiliarity with economics and overlook his clumsy administration for as long as they believe these traits are the prerequisite for his power in a crisis. But once the waters have calmed again and everyday problems reappear, then the statesman will have fulfilled his purpose and his tenure will usually come to an inglorious end.

It is as if the people who felt understood and supported by the statesman in a time of resistance and change then want to take revenge on the person they had relied upon in their weakness and timidity. When the tension borne of ambivalence between the statesman and his people abates, the once so ardent relationship suddenly evaporates into nothing. The statesman will lose the next election and go down in history for it.

We, the public, apparently can't get enough of such stories. It is revealing that political themes which are adopted for the purposes of presenting dubious characters, unfathomable passions, and complex learning processes enjoy enduring popularity in movies and, now more than ever before, in television shows. We need only think of Kevin Spacey as Francis Underwood in the American series *House of Cards*, or Sidse Babett Knudsen as Birgitte Nyborg in *Borgen* from Denmark. The great themes here are power, envy, sex, and prestige. These shows revolve around techniques of self-assertion, ways of concealing motives, and methods of calculating effectiveness in murky situations within multi-level worlds. Along with champions of self-esteem and masters of intrigue, we encounter stubborn, ignorant, and pathetic characters who try to come to terms with their lifelong fears, lifelong lies, and lifelong trembling. Power can apparently be dramatized in a more instructive and enthralling way in the world of politics than in that of economics or sports. The questions addressed for our entertainment are: Who rules us? Who do we follow? What do we believe?

This observation from the factory of mass media is confirmed by the sociology of celebrity.[11] The top spots on the celebrity scale are occupied not by figures from the world of entertainment or sports, or by the rich with their business successes and social projects; no, the uncontested leaders by a wide margin are the politicians who are considered to be the leaders of a country's politics – and out in front are the respective holders of the highest and most important public office.

Nothing interests the people on a talk show more than what the American president, the French president, or the German chancellor have to say about their motivations, convictions, and goals. Even former government leaders are invited to attend and speak at events for a great deal of money, and their mere physical presence is often more important than what they have to say about the state of the world. We want to know their aspirations and feelings so we can find out something about ourselves.

The fear of others

For many, however, the *we* proves to be fragmented and split. A powerful social fear holds sway in today's ethnically heterogeneous society, one which revolves around ourselves and the threat that seems to be posed by others. There is talk of a fear of foreign infiltration and even a fear of terror. But who is afraid of whom here?

In *Fear of Small Numbers*, a book written under the shadow of 9/11 and published in 2006 by Arjun Appadurai, an Indian-born globalization theorist living in the USA, Appadurai points out the pervasive anxiety regarding the incompleteness of our collective existence in societies of our kind. By societies of our kind, Appadurai means the societies in the OECD world. As long as the nation state was viewed as a self-evident container for modern society, one which promised a sufficient degree of social security to its inhabitants and the same political rights to its citizens despite unevenly distributed economic power, there was a framework for the unity of differences. Appadurai was thinking of the consolidated nation states in the post-1945 era, which moved past the violent processes of their unification by excluding foreign populations and embracing native ones.[1] Of course, even afterward there were disputes between established populations and newcomers which, according to Norbert Elias, were conducted with ugly blame-gossip and harsh rebukes. The power to define the criteria by which different life customs are valued is held by those who successfully assert their claim to have been there before the others who showed up later.[2] Power is secured through the authority to ascribe value. But over time, people became accustomed to a growing plurality of communities of "common descent,"[3] and they accepted the realities of mutual entanglements for the benefit of all. Italian restaurants, Greek tailors, Turkish metalworkers in the car industry, and Vietnamese eye doctors are part of the fabric of society. The shy, homesick "domestic foreigners"[4] who would meet in front of the train station on the weekends and keep to themselves with their fear that eats the soul have, in many cases, become perfectly normal citizens who finance their own homes and defend their children's secondary schools. In terms of exhaustion anxiety and educational panic, they are no different than their "domestically grown" neighbors in the same social situation.

The nation state was the roof under which social relationships were gradually restructured through the acceptance of other ways of life and new life energies. The generalization of value relations in the wake of the cultural upheaval of 1968, the expansion of entitlements through the grand coalition of social policy, and the internalization of comparative perspectives through tourism, pop culture, and TV shows created the conditions for the inclusion of citizens with very different migration stories.

But since nation states have found themselves compelled – through a complex interplay of purposeful liberalization from within and forced deregulation from without, which has come to be known as globalization – to open their borders to capital, information, goods, services and, ultimately, people, the lovely image of the gradual integration of outsiders and incremental change through others no longer seems tenable for the inhabitants of the perforated container. With the opening of the Iron Curtain, the expansion of the EU, and the establishment of refugee routes across the Mediterranean, an image has emerged among the middle class in the "postnational nation" of a fortress to be defended against "intruders." These intruders are thought to slip through holes in border fortifications and hide in the Trojan horses of refugee centers, and there seems to be no controlling them. The cry that goes up in the face of mass-media images of the plight of refugees – namely, that "we can't be the welfare office for the whole world!" – illustrates the irresolvable inner ambivalence between human compassion and human coldness. We see the lost souls striving to reach Europe from Africa in unseaworthy boats and we certainly don't want to blame them for their terrible fate, but we recoil at the idea of opening the floodgates to endless streams of migrants. Empathy for the individual is thus mixed with a fear of the mass.

For Appadurai, the fear of a population's incompleteness begets the horrors of cleansing and fortification. The defensive argument here usually mixes elements of demography, education, and culture. There are only a few of them now, so the argument goes, but there will be more and more because this hungry population has such a high birth rate. These are marginally qualified people, or so it's feared, who will put even more strain on our welfare system, which is already overloaded on account of our own restrained birth rates. These people are from a different cultural circle who close themselves off from their environment and will thus remain foreign bodies in our country. This minority is merely the precursor to a majority that will eventually push us to the margins. And we must therefore fend them off if we do not want to die out.

But the actual tipping point in our sense of security was the terrorist attack on the Twin Towers in New York City on September 11, 2001, which involved non-German students from Hamburg who had appeared entirely unremarkable up to that point. Who are these people living among us as sleepers for years, waiting to be deployed in the war against the West? In 2006, Hans Magnus Enzensberger speculated about the "radical losers" in a global social sorting process who are gripped by an agonizing feeling of aggrievement and humiliation which demands a grandiose expression of rage.[5] Ever since then, our relationship with strangers has been tied up with the fear of Islamic fundamentalism.

Muslims who identify themselves as such or are identified by others feel that they are suddenly being viewed as strangers in their own country. The headscarf question – when one dares pose it at all – can very quickly turn into a test of the emancipation level of a Muslim woman. "I am the way I am" is the only possible answer. This exoticization of the other changes the entire scene for the objects of this gaze. The looks thrown their way are not just suspicious, they harbor a latent fear. Without a single word being spoken, the other is forced into a position of having to justify himself. Can I help it if I look like a solemn Arab who has sworn allegiance to the suffering of his people? I am one, but I've lived in this country since I was five, and I've been a citizen since I turned 18.

Situations such as these bring into focus our fear of strangers in the crowd. The xenophobic gaze that sees immigrants as competitors in the fight for scarce resources has, since 9/11, merged with an underlying fear of Islam. Islam does not correspond to the image of the private and sentimental religion that seems appropriate to a functionally differentiated society with no center and no apex; instead, it presents itself as a public and naïve religion[6] to which one professes faith through signs that are visible to all, and which sets non-negotiable boundaries through definitive doctrines and precisely defined liturgical practices. Unlike the Catholic church, however – which also insists on codified rituals and requires its followers to repeatedly profess their faith in a loud voice in every Holy Mass – Islam resembles Protestant churches and dominions in that it does not recognize a supreme authority with a holy status. This gives rise to the outward impression that there is enough room within the framework of Islam for self-appointed radical interpreters who would not hesitate to declare a state of emergency against dissidents and enemies. In this case, the rule of God means self-rule against foreign rule.

The Muslim who naturally eats no pork and drinks no alcohol, who also fasts to a certain extent and never passes a beggar without giving alms, senses within himself the defiant inclination to appear to be how others expect him to be. For him, Islam is not a strict and rigid religion that one must obey absolutely, it is a way of life that does not ignore life's transcendental point of reference. Certain customs and practices can be of service here, which are naturally expressed all the more clearly the more one feels the pressure to live a leveled-out lifestyle of unaffectedness and abandon.

Why should I be understanding of the fears of those who have gone mad? What right do they have to expect me to make the first step toward understanding in a difficult situation? When will we have to stop justifying ourselves?

One side is afraid because it feels threatened by a minority, and the other because it feels threatened by the majority. And both sides, which have very unequal opportunities, suffer from a fear of the incompleteness of their collective existence. It is not possible to maintain the imaginary concept of an ethnically homogeneous milieu, however, either for the established majority or the minority that arrived later. Considering the fact that around half of all schoolchildren in major German cities have a migration background, neither the Germans of German descent nor those of non-German descent can keep to themselves in the long run. The Germans are no more of a self-contained unit than the Ottomans or Arabs or Europeans. These are ultimately abstract identifiers that are loaded with intense feeling but mask extremely variable concrete categorizations. If people insist on the idea of a collective *we* nonetheless, then the question is what new kind of social *we* will form in contrast to which *other* in an ethnically heterogeneous milieu.

The foremost aspect of this is that immigrants no longer want to be perceived as immigrants. Tuncay Acar, a musician and cultural events organizer who was born in Munich as the son of a Turkish "guest worker" and who founded the Göthe Protokoll network in his hometown, fumed on his blog when he heard about an art project in which a "person with a migration background" would guide spectators through an "immigrant neighborhood" of Munich: "Like hell am I going to explain my 'sketchy immigrant neighborhood' to you for the three thousand and five hundredth time! Am I a puppet or what? It's your neighborhood too, dammit. Just look at it. It's your country too, your city, your history..."[7]

It is obvious that the symmetry of fear evoked by terror requires a third position. This is only normatively defined – using the political vocabulary of trans-migrancy – by the term "people of color." At the moment, the focus is on not forbidding either of the two imagined sides to feel their fears. Then perhaps those involved will realize that the fear for themselves immediately provokes the fear of others.

Generational lessons

James Salter, who was born in 1925 and fought in World War II, opens his late work *All That Is* (first published in 2013) by describing situations of fear from the Second World War, as his 20-year-old protagonist is heading for the Japanese island of Okinawa with the American fleet:

> In tier on tier of iron bunks below deck, silent, six deep, lay hundreds of men, many faceup with their eyes still open though it was near morning. The lights were dimmed, the engines throbbing endlessly, the ventilators pulling in damp air, fifteen hundred men with their packs and weapons...[1]

In societies of our kind, no one is familiar anymore with this fear that was felt on a voyage to a foreign, unknown land to fight the decisive battle in a war that had dragged on for three and a half years.

> Courage and fear and how you would act under fire were not among the things you talked about.[2]

The surviving soldiers who fought in World War II and are now approaching 90 can talk about the silence surrounding fear in combat. They will do so laconically, signaling to listeners that the war was an experience they don't want to make any grand speeches about.

Salter's novel makes it clear that the fear didn't evaporate once the war was over. In the cool fifties and early sixties, the substitutes for fear were sex, alcohol, and a career. In this generation, which preferred John Coltrane, pop art, cybernetics, and the Atomium, it was ultimately the women who addressed the fear of fear.

Back in 1934, the German-born American psychoanalyst Karen Horney determined that any woman who ventured to have her own career would confront external and internal conflicts if she was not willing to pursue this venture at the cost of her femininity.[3] The patriarchal ideal of a woman who desires only to be loved by a man and to return his love, to admire him and serve him, had thus already died out before the war. In the postwar "mad men"[4] era, the psychological theories that adopted a woman's perspective used concepts of the female fear of fear to reveal men's wary defensiveness against women who were preparing to following them into their areas of performance.

The discovery from back then has become the reality of now. It was women who benefited from the expansion of education in the postwar period, as can be seen in the fact that young women have outnumbered young men in college for decades. And with their higher education degrees, they are also asserting a claim to professional positions once reserved for men. There is no turning back this wheel.

Nearly four decades after Karen Horney, Margarete

Mitscherlich went so far as to say that a newly won self-confidence on the part of women could also help men learn not to cling so desperately to sexual conquests and professional recognition. The more secure the new woman was within herself, Mitscherlich said, the greater her understanding for men and their fears. And men also had to realize that they would often construct a "false self" as part of their defense against emotions, fears, and desires for dependence.[5]

World War II is an important turning point in the history of the impact of fear in the twentieth century. On the one side are the generations who experienced the war in their youth and would rather not talk about the fear associated with the need to make fundamental decisions in borderline situations – because talking about it does no good anyway.[6] With their message that the worst is behind us, these generations seem practically fearless to their grandchildren and great-grandchildren.[7] Even for the wartime children born around 1940, the first postwar period brought with it an atmosphere of hostility, deprivation, isolation, and fear, from which this generation finally freed itself with great fanfare in 1968.

On the other side of the line are the generations who only know history as a history of more security, more comfort, more rights, and more opportunities. For them, the maximum credible accident has yet to materialize. Individual industriousness and caution can do nothing to counter such a danger. This means that the worst that can happen to everyone is not behind us, but in front of us. Harrisburg, Chernobyl, Sellafield, and, finally, Fukushima have given us an inkling of what such accidents might look like if they happened near

St. Etienne, Hamburg, Newcastle, or Helsinki. But for these cohorts of a long postwar period, fear arises first and foremost from the reference to assumptions which, like laws of nature, are thought to be ineluctable. For them, it is unthinkable that Germans would go to war against Russians, that pensions would be cut, that homosexuals would be denied jobs, or that the River Rhine would once again become a chemical cesspit. For all of the ambivalence toward progress – of which these generations are certainly aware – social conditions have, by and large, actually gotten better and not worse. The only conceivable end to this would be through eternal recurrence or random catastrophe. The base experience that determines the horizon of expectations of these postwar generations is no longer war, but a potentially deceptive peace that brings with it very different sources of fear.

Nonetheless, amalgamations of old and new fears are always possible. Following the national debt crisis in the Eurogroup and Russia's intervention in Ukraine, we can no longer expect Europe to stabilize itself internally in the wake of continual EU expansion. Instead, the rhetoric of mutual recrimination conveys the impression that the constellations of World War II – with their fears of retribution, inferiority complexes, and dependencies – are back on the table.

Deep-seated affective schematisms are coming to light, ones which cannot be called stereotypes because they are based on very real experiences of genocide, war, and displacement. These are mood complexes that can evidently be invoked immediately in tense social situations. Western and Eastern demagogues are only able to kindle them, however, because these fears are passed down through generations and form a latent horizon of expectations. Russification and Americanization after 1945 left behind tendencies toward demarcation and fantasies of self-determination throughout Europe, which are fed by a concealed desire for revenge stemming from the fact that European states were unable to liberate and protect themselves and therefore found themselves lacking the collective self-image of free and proud nations.

Fears are difficult to separate from one another because the lines of stimulation run together in the same direction, and all specific reasons for them dissolve in a diffuse desire to put the fears behind us and bring them to an end. This explains why, among the younger generations all over Europe who did not experience war and genocide or liberation and occupation, we see fanatic avenging angels emerging who conflate entirely different generational experiences[8] in such a way that it no longer seems possible to calmly examine the emotional triggers and sources of sentiment in the respective public social spheres.

Research into political culture basically offers two recommendations for dealing publicly with fear. One can be found in an oft-quoted essay by Franz L. Neumann from 1954 about the problem of anxiety in politics,[9] which explains how a society that had grown more abstract on account of the advanced division of labor and expanded marketization had become susceptible to regressive mass movements of fear. Anonymous systems of rules and unintended effects make the public more willing to follow the false concreteness of conspiracy theories and to blame scapegoats for everything that goes wrong. Neumann, who had been arrested as a Jew in Germany in 1933 but was able to emigrate to England in the same year, harked back to the experiences of the preceding decades, which had instilled in his readership a fear of the masses who, as he cautiously but unambiguously expressed, were capable of committing all manner of atrocities. The Caesar of today's society who could win over the masses would give a voice and direction to a politically homeless anti-capitalism.

Neumann recognized that every political system is based on the fundamental fear of standing alone, and that political communization in modern, sub-divided societies takes place by means of identifications that bring together isolated individuals. In principle, this can happen in a cooperative way when many similar individuals come together in a collective of shared ideas and binding interests. But for Neumann, the decisive affective identification is that of masses with leaders, which inevitably goes hand in hand with the deterioration and loss of the ego, and which empowers Caesarist leaders to employ despotism and violence against strangers and enemies in the name of the people.

The only defense against this, in Neumann's view, is to understand the reasons for the emergence of fear – reasons that can never be eliminated. The enlightened citizenry that can resist the temptation to overcome fear by coming together as a mass has acknowledged and accepted the psychologically fundamental fact of the irresolvable split between the ego and the world, the socially irreversible fact of alienation from work, and the politically insurmountable fact of competition between groups. The identifications that are nevertheless necessary for a living democracy should relate to organizations and should involve principles.

Parliamentarianism is one form of organization, and the "constitutional patriotism"[10] that was brought into play much later by Dolf Sternberger and promoted by Jürgen Habermas[11] is one principle for a form of political identification that is free of the direct pressure of fear. There is no mistaking the desire for a political aesthetics of debate, constitution, and office here. Neumann introduced the inherently contradictory term "non-affective identification,"[12] which is apparently meant to describe a rationally tamed and intellectually conveyed enthusiasm. This would be based on a fear without fear, which would presumably be taught in certain educational institutions dedicated to the experience of the person as a whole.

A very different way of dealing publicly with fear was discovered in the culture of laughter in the Middle Ages, which was studied by the Russian literary theorist Mikhail Bakhtin, who died in Moscow in 1975 at the age of 80.[13] Bakhtin was interested in folk culture as it was expressed through carnival, the comic elements of mystery plays, ambiguous animal epics, bacchic prandial songs, and bawdy farces. We must imagine a drama of the body dealing with conception, birth, growth and infirmity, eating and drinking, and bodily excretions. The focus was not on the individual body and private life, however, but on the great body of the species and the people, for whom birth and death were not an absolute beginning and absolute end but simply moments in a comprehensive process of return and renewal. This process has cosmic aspects, and it melds with the image of a devouring and birthing Mother Earth.

Bakhtin emphasizes, first, the universalism of this culture of laughter, which flouts all that is forbidden and proscribed; second, its essential connection to the freedom that created space in the festive liberation of laughter and the body, and which stood in stark contrast to the ascetic rules of fasting and abstinence; and, third, its link to the non-official and non-serious truth of the people. Power, violence, and authority not only do not permit themselves to laugh – from the people's perspective, all of their seriousness makes it impossible for them to laugh in the first place.

Medieval man perceived laughter to be a victory over fear. This was not just a victory over the mystical fear conjured up in the cathedrals and churches (the "fear of God") or the fear of natural catastrophe; it was, above all, a victory over the moral fear that enslaves, oppresses, and dulls the consciousness of man. Everything threatening is made comical, everything terrifying is pushed into the grotesque, and in the hell of carnival, violence loses its horror.

Medieval laughter had nothing to do with the art of the subtle smile. It was not an expression of personal restraint but rather the rousing manifestation of a people's way of life. The carnival mass leveled out social differences by bringing individual bodies into contact with unfamiliar bodies of every age and social standing, with which they coalesced without shame or defenses.

Bakhtin, who was forced to spend 30 years in exile far from the centers of Russian intellectual life at the behest of Stalin, celebrates medieval laughter as the dissident sovereignty of the people. To the extent that it conquered the fear of hidden secrets, the impenetrable world, and unchallenged power, medieval laughter exposed the truth about power and oppression, authority and glory. It opposed lies, adulation, flattery, and

hypocrisy, and it did so by trusting in a truth that combined the feeling of eternal life with the belief that there
could be a different future.

So while Franz L. Neumann, who came from the
world of critical theory, counted on educating people
against fear in the belief that understanding would bring
wisdom, Mikhail Bakhtin, who worked in the tradition
of Russian Formalism, argued for using a playful, rebellious folk tradition as the antidote to the fear that robs
individuals of courage. What the two have in common
is the awareness of a certain anthropological expansive-
ness as a condition for the possibility of a public culture
of tempering fears of decline, status panic, and isolation-
ist tendencies. Fear is part of the reality of humankind,
though the constitution of medieval humanity was
very different from that of the sensitive souls of today.
Carnival is still celebrated and still considered to be an
extraordinary state of affairs in its respective strong-
holds – but today we also have psychoanalysis, Gestalt
therapy, and adventure tourism as additional arenas
for overcoming fear. Knowledge can open our minds,
laughter can liberate us, but the fear that everything is
going down the drain always harbors the question of a
different understanding of our situation.

Two years after the publication of David Riesman's
The Lonely Crowd, Paul Tillich's lectures were also
published in the USA in the book *The Courage To Be*.[14]
In this work, the Protestant theologian – who had emi-
grated to the USA in 1933 after being dismissed from his
civil service job at Johann Wolfgang Goethe University
in Frankfurt – explored potential ways of being oneself
in the face of an anxiety that is experienced as a narrow-
ness with no way out or an openness with no direction.

Without mentioning him by name, Tillich shares Riesman's analysis that the individual of today moves in a closed world of communication. The triumphal march of liberalism and democracy, the rise of a technical civilization, and the spread of a historicist culture have brought forth a society that is nothing more than society. Reference to others has taken the place of reference to a cosmic natural order or hidden soul. But other people are both heaven and hell: they can build me up and strengthen me with their approval, encouragement, and empathy, but their rejection, resentment, and dissociation can also unsettle and destroy me. The other-directed character has nothing but the others who give him a footing in life and convey a concept of his selfhood. The root of fear comes from this ineluctable orientation toward an instance that is just as insecure, unstable, and unpredictable as the others who are fundamentally closed to me. Since that which applies to me always applies to the others as well, we are – as sociologists would say – dealing with conditions of double contingency that mean every act of communication has us skating on thin ice.

The fear that we could break through and fall into a hole in our being at any moment is expressed in two existential attempts to escape, according to Tillich: you either want to retreat from others or throw yourself into their arms. Buddhism would be the way out in the former case, conformism in the latter.[15] Buddhist mysticism seeks a state beyond disappointment and non-disappointment in the pure here and now, which cannot be relativized against anything else. The single-note music of John Cage, the blue of Yves Klein, the purely random movements of Merce Cunningham, and the Case Study Houses of Charles and Ray Eames are examples of this kind of Buddhism, in which fear is dissolved by leaping into nothingness.

Losing oneself in the conformism of the "lonely crowd" is the other way out. The radar character follows the fashions, pleasures, excitements, and resentments of others with the indifference that is required to be able to catch the next wave that comes along. External participation without internal involvement is the method used here to rid oneself of the fear for oneself.

According to Tillich, both emptying oneself and filling oneself serve only to numb the fear of becoming aware that communication is everything, but it is based on nothing. "Meaning is saved, but the self is sacrificed."[16]

But none of this is of any use, in Tillich's opinion. Neither cynical disdain, skeptical arrogance nor ascetic purification can eliminate the question of how one can be a part of something from which one is separated at the same time. The self that retreats into its own four walls to find peace is just as susceptible to feelings of meaninglessness and emptiness as the self that comes together with random others in a square to claim its own public space. This is because there is always a danger that both things will be lost: participation in our shared world along with our individual self. Communication happens without our willing it and outside of our control, but it takes courage to surrender to this if you want to feel like yourself and find yourself with and through and in this uncertain and open communicative back-and-forth.

Without others there is no self, without ambiguity there is no identity, without desperation there is no hope, without an end there is no beginning. And in between, we find fear.

If you seek to escape this or place yourself above it, you have given in to fear. In his total resignation, Socrates – who recognizes that in all ability there is inability, in all knowledge there is ignorance, and in all being there is a nothingness, and who thus dies serenely for his convictions – would appear to have conquered fear. But with his superior smile, this philosopher of "obscene questioning"[17] has lost the sense of a life which, by repeatedly revealing itself and losing its orientation for a moment, lives itself. Fear debunks the life lies of happiness, glamour, and fame, but for Tillich it also preserves the hope – however trembling and tentative – that nothing must stay the way it is.

Notes

Fear as a principle

1 Luhmann, *Ecological Communication*, p. 128.
2 Wildt, *An Uncompromising Generation*.
3 Franklin D. Roosevelt, "Inaugural Address, March 4, 1933," pp. 11–16.
4 Kaufmann, *Sicherheit als soziologisches und sozial-politisches Problem*.
5 Roosevelt in conversation with the journalist Anne O'Hare McCormick in the *New York Times Magazine*; McCormick, "The two men at the big moment," pp. 1f.
6 This is borne out by surveys conducted among young women on behalf of the magazine *Brigitte*, for example; Allmendinger, "Frauen auf dem Sprung."
7 Regarding the concept of social exclusion that cuts across the social status system, see Bude, *Die Ausgeschlossenen*.
8 Kierkegaard, *The Concept of Anxiety*, p. 42.
9 This is the message in a global bestseller writ-

ten by a Nobel Prize winner in economics: Daniel Kahneman, *Thinking, Fast and Slow*.

10 In her book *On Death and Dying*, Elisabeth Kübler-Ross defines five phases of dying – denial, anger, bargaining, depression and, finally, acceptance – which can be considered "productive" strategies for coping with an extremely stressful situation.

11 This term (in German: *Egotaktiker*) was coined in 2002 by Klaus Hurrelmann in the 14th Shell German Youth Survey to characterize the generation of 12- to 15-year-olds who seemed as geared toward security and achievement as their parents, but who appeared to be largely unmoved by wider political issues.

12 In Wilhelmine Germany, the Catholic church and social democracy represented sustaining "loser cultures" because they sent a message to those who were denied access and suffered degradation that what happened to them as individuals was not their problem alone, but rather the expression of a collective life situation.

13 Damitz, "Prekarität: Genealogie einer Problemdiagnose."

14 In literature, the genre for this form of self-socialization is the bildungsroman – following Goethe's *Wilhelm Meister's Apprenticeship* from 1795 to 1796 and *Wilhelm Meister's Journeyman Years* from 1821 and 1829.

15 Riesman/Denney/Glazer, *The Lonely Crowd*, p. 18.

16 Cicourel, "Basic and Normative Rules."

17 Riesman/Denney/Glazer, *The Lonely Crowd*, p. 22.

18 The classic works here include Ted R. Gurr, *Why*

Men Rebel, and Walter G. Runciman, *Relative Deprivation and Social Justice.*

19 Hobfoll, "Conservation of Resources."

20 For Harry Stack Sullivan (*The Interpersonal Theory of Psychiatry*), who was one of the first to identify the importance of social experience in the development of mental disorders, the personification of self that dies a social death is not the "good-me" who appeals to others nor the "bad-me" who is undesirable, but rather the "not-me" who simply fades away.

Longing for a non-terminable relationship

1 Laing/Phillipson/Lee, *Interpersonal Perception*, p. 27.

2 Goffman, *Asylums.*

3 This is Isaiah Berlin's famous distinction between "Two Concepts of Liberty."

4 This expression was coined by Heinrich Popitz in his analysis of power relations; *Phenomena of Power*, pp. 25ff.

5 Blinky Palermo (Peter Heisterkamp), 1943–1977, German abstract painter.

6 For example, speed-daters who search for the optimal partner by continually liaising with new people are more likely to end up alone than the wall flowers who are less sociable but more devoted to their relationships. See Konrad, "Affection, Speed Dating and Heartbreaking."

7 Buber, *I and Thou.*

8 Such as Rüdiger Peuckert, *Familienformen im sozialen Wandel.*

9 Mephistopheles speaking to Faust in *Faust: Part I* by Johann Wolfgang von Goethe.

10 Horst-Eberhard Richter (*Eltern, Kind und Neurose*) had already encountered these scenarios.

Unease with one's own type

1 Hans Peter Dreitzel (*Die Einsamkeit als soziologisches Problem*) views this as the constitutive loneliness of the social climber.
2 Packard, *The Status Seekers*.
3 This theory can be traced back to Robert K. Merton, "Contributions to the Theory of Reference Group Behavior."
4 Parsons, "Certain Primary Sources and Patterns of Aggression in the Social Structure of the Western World," pp. 298–322.

When the winners take it all

1 An overwhelming flood of literature now exists on this basic concept in the interpretation of modern life; see, e.g., Erika Fischer-Lichte, *Ästhetik der Performanz*, or the article "Performanz" by Aldo Legnaro, pp. 204–9.
2 See, e.g., Hans Peter Dreitzel, *Elitebegriff und Sozialstruktur*, pp. 99ff., which, in turn, is based on the classic study by Gustav Ichheiser, *Kritik des Erfolges*.
3 In this respect, the theory of the dominance of success without performance, which is characteristic of neoliberalism, is only half the story; see Neckel, *Flucht nach vorn*.
4 Scheler, *Ressentiment*, p. 4.
5 Adorno, *The Authoritarian Personality*, pp. 685ff.
6 This is how Micha Brumlik ("Charakter, Habitus

und Emotion," pp. 141–54) accurately characterized the sociology of Pierre Bourdieu.

7 Wurmser, *The Mask of Shame.*

8 The psychiatrist Michael Linden says that "posttraumatic embitterment disorder" can arise as a
potential reaction to extreme but common stressors
such as dismissal, separation, or loss if these life
events are felt to be extremely unjust, grievous, or
degrading. It leads to lasting feelings of bitterness
combined with feelings of helplessness, self-blame
and blaming others, and destructive fantasies. It
often ends with the sufferer punishing the supposed
aggressor through self-destructive behavior.

The status panic of the middle class

1 Kierkegaard, *The Concept of Anxiety*, p. 42.

2 Ibid., p. 44, emphasis in original.

3 We must not forget the social advancement of large
portions of the population after 1945. Taking into
account both the "old" and "new middle class" as
defined by Theodor Geiger (*Die soziale Schichtung*),
around one third of the German population could be
considered middle class in the mid-1920s, while in
the 1960s nearly half of the people in West Germany
resided in the middle-class comfort zone, if we take
into account the upper-, middle-, and lower-middle
classes as defined by Karl-Martin Bolte et al. (*Soziale
Schichtung*). This is according to Stefan Hradil,
Soziale Ungleichheit in Deutschland, pp. 365 and
357.

4 Berger/Offe, "Das Rationalisierungsdilemma der
Angestelltenarbeit," pp. 271–90.

5 Kracauer, *The Salaried Masses*, p. 30.

6 Regarding this social physiognomy, see Mau, *Lebenschancen.*

7 This is a fitting expression from Michel Foucault (*Technologies of the Self*), which emphasizes the fact that the middle-class self goes to great lengths to become what it wants to be in accordance with certain aesthetic values and criteria of style.

8 Dahrendorf, *The Modern Social Conflict*, p. 112.

9 Dahrendorf, "Die globale Klasse," pp. 1057–68.

10 Hradil/Schmidt, "Angst und Chancen," p. 203.

11 Herfried Münkler (*Mitte und Maß*, pp. 51ff.) points out the growing refractoriness of higher earners whose expectations have been frustrated.

12 Geiger, "Panik im Mittelstand," pp. 637–54.

13 Regarding this concept, see the Caritas study conducted in the 1990s by Hübinger (*Prekärer Wohlstand*), who originally looked at (male and female) skilled workers, low-level employees, and low-grade civil servants.

14 Beck, *Risk Society*, pp. 85ff.

15 This metaphor comes from Annette Pehnt, *Lexikon der Angst*, p. 107.

16 In connection with this, see also Hradil/Schmidt, "Angst und Chancen," p. 214.

17 Dominic Wilson and Raluca Dragusanu, "The Expanding Middle: The Exploding World Middle Class and Falling Global Inequality," quoted in Mau, *Lebenschancen*, p. 64.

18 Regarding this, see Bude, *Bildungspanik.*

19 The negative results of the first PISA (Programme for International Student Assessment) survey in 2000 led to a reform of the German school system.

20 The two references here are Reich, *The Work*

of Nations, with his concept of systems analysis competencies, and Bourdieu, *Distinction*, with his concept of a profit of distinction.

21 Mills, *White Collar*.

Everyday battles on the lower rungs

1 See, e.g., Evers/Nowotny, *Über den Umgang mit Unsicherheit*, or Ewald, *L'Etat providence*.

2 The notion that, in worlds of similarity, uniqueness is based on the tiniest differences has been familiar in sociology since the classic works of scholars such as Thorstein Veblen and Georg Simmel.

3 The following account is based on two important new studies of the situation of the "service proletariat" in Germany by Friederike Bahl, *Lebensmodelle in der Dienstleistungsgesellschaft*, and Philipp Staab, *Macht und Herrschaft in der Servicewelt*.

4 The data on this employment segment comes from Oesch, *Redrawing the Class Map*, p. 126.

5 This doesn't rule out the possibility of packages being in transit for a week because they've inexplicably been transferred from one private delivery firm to another.

6 Baumol, "Macroeconomics of Unbalanced Growth," pp. 416–26.

7 Oesch calculated that a total of 62 percent of the people employed in routine services are women, while 80 percent of the equal-ranking industrial workforce is male (see Oesch, *Redrawing the Class Map*, p. 88).

8 According to Oesch, only 18 percent of these employees are members of a trade union, whereas the figure for "routine" industrial workers is 39

percent (Oesch, *Redrawing the Class Map*, p. 168).

The fragile self

1 The relevant literature has been compiled by Summer, *Macht die Gesellschaft depressiv?*
2 Sennett, *The Fall of Public Man*; id., *Authority*; and id., *The Corrosion of Character*; Lasch, *The Culture of Narcissism*; Giddens, *The Transformation of Intimacy*; and, finally, the books by Ehrenberg, *The Weariness of the Self* and *La société du malaise*.
3 Ehrenberg, *La société du malaise* [The Uneasy Society], p. 13.
4 This is how Ralf Dahrendorf expressed it in his summary of sociological role theory, "Homo Sociologicus," p. 22.
5 Schultz-Hencke, *Der gehemmte Mensch*.
6 Berger/Luckmann, *The Social Construction of Reality*.
7 This is a summary of the results of an international survey (in the USA, Brazil, Singapore, and Switzerland) among young people between the ages of 16 and 25, which was conducted by Markus Freitag from the Institute of Political Science at the University of Bern on behalf of Credit Suisse; see Bulletin No. 4, 2013, pp. 29–51. The results clearly show that, despite this generation's evident aversion to xenophobia and ethnocentrism, it is less willing to accept disruptions and impairments in its own environment. The affirmation of values such as empathy and tolerance in this age group goes hand in hand with a readiness to condemn graffiti as criminal property damage and to install video cameras to identify uninvited visitors.

8 See Bude, "Zum Problem der Selbstdetermination," pp. 84–111.

9 Following Viktor von Weizsäcker, see Albert Zacher, "The Case History and the 'Unlived Life,'" pp. 1073–6.

10 See Vogl, *On Tarrying*, who explores every facet of this fundamental attitude of reservation toward things that are the way they are.

11 Kunkel, *Indecision*. Incidentally, Benjamin Kunkel was one of the initial contributors to the American literary magazine *n+1*, which bills itself as a journal of the zeitgeist. See Kunkel/Gessen (eds.), *Ein Schritt weiter*.

Rule by nobody

1 The 2012 Harris Poll Annual RQ Public Summary Report: A Survey of the U.S. General Public Using the Reputation Quotient.

2 This image was used in the article "Obama, Merkel, and the Bridge to an Information Civilization" by Shoshana Zuboff, an American economist and author of *In the Age of the Smart Machine*, a groundbreaking book published in 1988 about how information technology changes the way we work.

3 The browser is Mozilla Firefox, whose advertising slogan in February 2014 was "Doing good is part of our code."

4 We need look no further than the strange evidence rooms of the Stasi in East Germany, with their stuck-together audio tapes and sealed odor samples.

5 Deleuze, "Control and Becoming," p. 175.

6 Deleuze/Guattari, *A Thousand Plateaus*.

7 Watzlawick/Bavelas/Jackson, *The Pragmatics of Human Communication.*

8 "What the networker misses," Urs Stäheli notes, "is the ability to cap connections, tolerate failed connections, or even strive for and enjoy non-connection." See Stäheli, "Entnetzt euch! Praktiken und Ästhetiken der Anschlusslosigkeit," p. 4.

9 The author of the article, Evgeny Morozov, was born in Belarus in 1984 and lives in the USA. He contributes a column, "Silicon Valley," to the *Frankfurter Allgemeine Zeitung* newspaper; quote from: "Why we are allowed to hate Silicon Valley."

10 "A new global depression?", interview with Richard Duncan.

11 Postberg, *Macht und Geld*, p. 135.

12 See Reifner, *Die Geldgesellschaft*, pp. 15ff.

13 The following considerations are based on insights into the practical logic of money found in a work published recently by Aaron Sahr, *Das Versprechen des Geldes*, about the role of credit in modern capitalism.

14 Böckenförde, "Woran der Kapitalismus krankt."

15 Minsky, "The Financial-Instability Hypothesis," p. 25.

16 This is the tenor of more recent sociological theories of money based on Schumpeter and Keynes. The door to this debate was opened by Ingham, "On the Underdevelopment of the Sociology of Money."

17 This expression was coined by Arendt, *The Human Condition*, who viewed the "rule by nobody" as a contemporary type of conformist rule. Arendt, like more recent financial market theorists, was talking

about a conformity of the herd which can take effect even if it has not been explicitly agreed upon.

The power of emotion

1 By this, Popitz means the characteristic forms of expression of one and the same person, or self-assertion in the floating fluctuation of social roles; cf. Popitz, "The Concept of Social Role as an Element of Sociological Theory."

2 As strongly emphasized by Luhmann, *Ecological Communication*.

3 Egbert/Bergmann, "Angst – Von der Phänomenologie zur Interaktion."

4 Schulz, "Das Problem der Angst in der neueren Philosophie."

5 Heidegger's student Ernst Tugendhat (*Egocentricity and Mysticism*) used this idea as the basis for developing a contemporary form of mysticism.

6 Kirsch/Mackscheidt, *Staatsmann, Demagoge, Amtsinhaber*.

7 Ibid., p. 11.

8 Marine Le Pen of the *Front National* in France and Pia Kjærsgaard of the *Dansk Folkeparti* in Denmark are evidence that female demagogues are on the advance in the twenty-first century under the banner of "welfare state chauvinism."

9 Adorno, "Freudian Theory and the Pattern of Fascist Propaganda," p. 134.

10 Kirsch/Mackscheidt, *Staatsmann, Demagoge, Amtsinhaber*, p. 85.

11 Peters, *Prominenz*.

The fear of others

1 Regarding the common origin of functional differentiation and national identification, see Bielefeld, *Nation und Gesellschaft.*
2 Elias/Scotson, *The Established and the Outsiders.*
3 This expression ("*Abstammungsgemeinschaft*") is from Weber, "Ethnic Groups."
4 Bielefeld, *Inländische Ausländer.*
5 Enzensberger, "The Terrorist Mindset: The Radical Loser."
6 This distinction rightly calls to mind the difference between Protestantism and Catholicism in Christianity. See Bude, "Die Zukunft der Religion."
7 Quoted in Dössel, "Die Ausgeschlossenen."

Generational lessons

1 Salter, *All That Is*, p. 3.
2 Ibid., p. 9.
3 Horney, "The Overvaluation of Love," p. 183.
4 Reference to the American TV series, with characters from the lonely crowd who, in the early 1960s, act in confinement and dream of breaking out.
5 Mitscherlich, "Emanzipation und Sexualität der Frau," p. 53.
6 Regarding the cohort of student soldiers in World War II, see Bude, *Deutsche Karrieren*, or Schörken, *Luftwaffenhelfer und Drittes Reich.*
7 In Germany, Helmut Schmidt – who was born in 1918 and, while serving as German chancellor, refused to release Red Army Faction members held in custody in exchange for the kidnapped Hanns Martin Schleyer, and who also asserted NATO's double-track decision in the face of fierce opposition

in West German society – is viewed as the exemplary virtuoso of the fear of world war.

8 Faimberg, "The Telescoping of Generations."
9 Neumann, "Anxiety and Politics."
10 Sternberger, "Verfassungspatriotismus."
11 See, e.g., Habermas, "Historical Consciousness and Post-Traditional Identity."
12 Neumann, "Anxiety and Politics," p. 278.
13 Bakhtin, *Rabelais and His World.*
14 Tillich, *The Courage to Be.*
15 This follows the thinking of Klaus Heinrich (*Versuch über die Schwierigkeit nein zu sagen*), who was probably Tillich's most important German disciple.
16 Tillich, *The Courage to Be*, p. 49.
17 Bodenheimer, *Warum? Von der Obszönität des Fragens.*

Bibliography

"A new global depression?" Interview with Richard Duncan, *New Left Review* 77, September–October 2012. Available online at https://newleftreview.org/II/77/richard-duncan-a-new-global-depression

Adorno, Theodor W. (1985): "Freudian Theory and the Pattern of Fascist Propaganda" in Arato, Andrew/Gebhardt, Eike (eds.): *The Essential Frankfurt School Reader*. New York: Continuum, pp. 118–37. [*Die Freudsche Theorie und die Struktur der faschistischen Propaganda*, 1951]

Adorno, Theodor W./Frenkel-Brunswik, Else/Levinson, Daniel/Sanford, R. Nevitt (1950): *The Authoritarian Personality*. New York: Harper.

Allmendinger, Jutta (2009): *Frauen auf dem Sprung. Wie junge Frauen heute leben wollen. Die BRIGITTE-Studie*. Munich: Pantheon Verlag.

Appadurai, Arjun (2006): *Fear of Small Numbers: An Essay on the Geography of Anger*. Durham, NC: Duke University Press.

Arendt, Hannah (1998 [1958]): *The Human*

Condition. Chicago, IL: University of Chicago Press.

Bahl, Friederike (2014): *Lebensmodelle in der Dienstleistungsgesellschaft.* Hamburg: Hamburger Edition.

Bakhtin, Mikhail (1968): *Rabelais and His World.* Translated by Hélène Iswolsky. Cambridge, MA: MIT Press. [*Tvorchestvo Fransua Rable*, 1965]

Baumol, William J. (1967): "Macroeconomics of Unbalanced Growth: The Anatomy of Urban Crisis" *American Economic Review*, 57(3), 416–26.

Beck, Ulrich (2005): *Risk Society: Towards a New Modernity.* Translated by Mark Ritter. London: Sage Publications. [*Risikogesellschaft. Auf dem Weg in eine andere Moderne*, 1986]

Berger, Peter L./Luckmann, Thomas (1966): *The Social Construction of Reality: A Treatise in the Sociology of Knowledge.* Garden City, NY: Doubleday.

Berger, Ulrike/Offe, Claus (1984): "Das Rational-isierungsdilemma der Angestelltenarbeit" in Offe, Claus (ed.): *"Arbeitsgesellschaft": Strukturprobleme und Zukunftsperspektiven.* Frankfurt am Main: Campus.

Berlin, Isaiah (1969 [1958]): "Two Concepts of Liberty" in *Four Essays on Liberty.* Oxford: Oxford University Press, pp. 118–72.

Bielefeld, Ulrich (1988): *Inländische Ausländer. Zum gesellschaftlichen Bewusstsein türkischer Jugendlicher in der Bundesrepublik.* Frankfurt am Main: Campus.

Bielefeld, Ulrich (2003): *Nation und Gesellschaft. Selbstthematisierungen in Deutschland und Frankreich.* Hamburg: Hamburger Edition.

Böckenförde, Ernst-Wolfgang (2009): "Woran der

Kapitalismus krankt. Er krankt an seiner Grundidee. Notwendig ist eine Umkehrung des Ausgangspunktes" *Süddeutsche Zeitung*, April 13, p. 8.

Bodenheimer, Aron R. (1986): *Warum? Von der Obszönität des Fragens*. Stuttgart: Reclam.

Bolte, Karl Martin/Kappe, Dieter/Neidhardt, Friedhelm (1966): *Soziale Schichtung*. Opladen: Leske.

Bourdieu, Pierre (2010): *Distinction: A Social Critique of the Judgement of Taste*. Translated by Richard Nice. Cambridge, MA: Harvard University Press [*La Distinction: Critique sociale du judgement*, 1979]

Brumlik, Micha (2009): "Charakter, Habitus und Emotion oder die Möglichkeit von Erziehung? Zu einer Leerstelle im Werk Pierre Bourdieus" in Friebertshäuser, Barbara/Rieger-Ladich, Markus/Wigger, Lothar (eds.): *Reflexive Erziehungswissenschaft. Forschungsperspektiven im Anschluss an Pierre Bourdieu*. Wiesbaden: VS Verlag, pp. 141–54.

Buber, Martin (2000): *I and Thou*. Translated by Ronald Gregor Smith. New York: Scribner. [*Ich und Du*, 1923]

Bude, Heinz (1986): "Zum Problem der Selbstdetermination" in Soeffner, Hans-Georg (ed.): *Sozialstruktur und soziale Typik*. Frankfurt am Main: Campus, pp. 84–111.

Bude, Heinz (1987): *Deutsche Karrieren. Lebenskonstruktionen sozialer Aufsteiger aus der Falkhelfer-Generation*. Frankfurt am Main: edition suhrkamp.

Bude, Heinz (1997): *Das Altern einer Generation. Die Jahrgänge 1938–1948*. Frankfurt am Main: Suhrkamp.

Bude, Heinz (1999): "Die Zukunft der Religion" in

Bude, Heinz (ed.): *Die ironische Nation. Soziologie als Zeitdiagnose.* Hamburg: Hamburger Edition, pp. 123–38.

Bude, Heinz (2010): *Die Ausgeschlossenen. Das Ende vom Traum einer gerechten Gesellschaft.* Munich: Hanser Verlag.

Bude, Heinz (2011): *Bildungspanik. Was unsere Gesellschaft spaltet.* Munich: Hanser Verlag.

Cicourel, Aaron (1972): "Basic and Normative Rules in the Negotiation of Status and Role" in Sudow, David (ed.): *Studies in Social Interaction.* New York: The Free Press, pp. 229–58.

Dahrendorf, Ralf (1968): "Homo Sociologicus: On the History, Significance, and Limits of the Category of Social Role." Translated from the original German by the author, in *Essays in the Theory of Society.* Stanford, CA: Stanford University Press. [*Homo Sociologicus*, 1958]

Dahrendorf, Ralf (1990 [1988]): *The Modern Social Conflict: An Essay on the Politics of Liberty.* Berkeley, CA: University of California Press.

Dahrendorf, Ralf (2000): "Die globale Klasse und die neue Ungleichheit" *Merkur*, 54(11), 1057–68.

Damitz, Ralf (2007): "Prekarität. Genealogie einer Problemdiagnose" *Mittelweg 36*, 4(16), 67–86.

Deleuze, Gilles (1995): "Control and Becoming" in *Negotiations: 1972–1990.* Translated by Martin Joughin. New York: Columbia University Press, pp. 169–76. [*Pourparlers*, 1990]

Deleuze, Gilles/Guattari, Félix (2002): *A Thousand Plateaus: Capitalism and Schizophrenia.* Translated by Brian Massumi. London: Continuum. [*Mille Plateaux*, 1980]

Bibliography

Dössel, Christine (2014): "Die Ausgeschlossenen" *Süddeutsche Zeitung*, March 7, p. HF2.

Dreitzel, Hans Peter (1962): *Elitebegriff und Sozialstruktur. Eine soziologische Begriffsanalyse*. Stuttgart: Enke.

Dreitzel, Hans Peter (1970): *Die Einsamkeit als soziologisches Problem*. Zurich: Verlag der Arche.

Egbert, Maria/Bergmann, Jörg (2004): "Angst – Von der Phänomenologie zur Interaktion" *ZiF-Mitteilungen* 4, 1–12.

Ehrenberg, Alain (2010a): *La société du malaise: Le mental et la social*. Paris: Odile Jacob.

Ehrenberg, Alain (2010b): *The Weariness of the Self: Diagnosing the History of Depression in the Contemporary Age*. Translated by Enrico Caouette, Jacob Homel, David Homel, and Don Winkler. Kingston: McGill-Queen's University Press. [*La fatigue d'être soi: Dépression et société*, 1998]

Elias, Norbert/Scotson, John L. (1965): *The Established and the Outsiders: A Sociological Enquiry into Community Problems*. London: Frank Cass.

Enzensberger, Hans Magnus (2006): "The Terrorist Mindset: The Radical Loser" *SPIEGEL Magazine*, December 20. Translated by Nicholas Grindell. Available online at http://www.spiegel.de/internat ional/spiegel/the-terrorist-mindset-the-radical-loser-a-451379.html. [*Schreckens Männer*, 2006]

Evers, Adalbert/Nowotny, Helga (1987): *Über den Umgang mit Unsicherheit*. Frankfurt am Main: Suhrkamp.

Ewald, François (1986): *L'Etat providence*. Paris: B. Grasset.

Faimberg, Haydée (2005): "The Telescoping of

Generations: A Genealogy of Alienated Identifications" in *The Telescoping of Generations: Listening to the Narcissitic Links Between Generations*. London: Routledge, pp. 4–18. ["El telescopaje de generaciones," 1985]

Fischer-Lichte, Erika (2004): *Ästhetik der Performanz*. Frankfurt am Main: Suhrkamp.

Foucault, Michel (1988): *Technologies of the Self: A Seminar with Michel Foucault*. Amherst, MA: University of Massachusetts Press.

Frank, Robert H./Cook, Philip J. (1995): *The Winner-Take-All-Society: Why the Few at the Top Get So Much More Than the Rest of Us*. New York: Penguin Books.

Geiger, Theodor (1930): "Panik im Mittelstand" *Die Arbeit. Zeitschrift für Gewerkschaftspolitik und Wirtschaftskunde*, 7(10), 637–54.

Geiger, Theodor (1987 [1932]): *Die soziale Schichtung des deutschen Volkes. Soziographischer Versuch auf statistischer Grundlage* [The Social Stratification of the German People], facsimile of 1st edition. Stuttgart: Enke.

Giddens, Anthony (1992): *The Transformation of Intimacy: Sexuality, Love and Eroticism in Modern Societies*. Cambridge: Polity.

Goffman, Erving (1961): *Asylums: Essays on the Social Situation of Mental Patients and Other Inmates*. New York: Anchor Books.

Groh-Samberg, Olaf/Hertel, Florian R. (2010): "Abstieg aus der Mitte? Zur langfristigen Mobilität von Armut und Wohlstand" in Burzan, Nicole/Berger, Peter A. (eds.): *Dynamiken (in) der gesellschaftlichen Mitte*. Wiesbaden: Springer VS, pp. 138–57.

Bibliography

Gurr, Ted R. (1970): *Why Men Rebel*. Princeton, NJ: Princeton University Press.

Habermas, Jürgen (1989): "Historical Consciousness and Post-Traditional Identity: The Federal Republic's Orientation to the West" in *The New Conservativism: Cultural Criticism and the Historians' Debate*. Edited and translated by Shierry Weber Nicholson. Cambridge: Polity, pp. 249–67. [*Geschichtsbewußtsein und posttraditionale Identität*, 1987]

Heinrich, Klaus (1982 [1964]): *Versuch über die Schwierigkeit nein zu sagen*. Frankfurt am Main: Suhrkamp.

Herbert, Ulrich, Best (1996): *Biographische Studien über Radikalismus, Weltanschauung und Vernunft 1903–1989*. Bonn: Dietz.

Hermann, Ulrike (2010): *Hurra, wir dürfen zahlen. Der Selbstbetrug der Mittelschicht*. Frankfurt: Westend.

Hobfoll, Stevan E. (1989): "Conservation of Resources: A Critical Review of Evidence" *American Psychologist*, 44, 513–24.

Horney, Karen (1967 [1934]): "The Overvaluation of Love: A Study of a Common Present-day Feminine Type" in Kelman, Harold (ed.): *Feminine Psychology*. New York: W.W. Norton, pp. 182–213.

Hradil, Stefan (2001): *Soziale Ungleichheit in Deutschland*. Opladen: Leske + Budrich.

Hradil, Stefan/Schmidt, Holger (2007): "Angst und Chancen. Zur Lage der gesellschaftlichen Mitte aus soziologischer Sicht" in Herbert-Quandt-Stiftung (ed.): *Zwischen Erosion und Erneuerung. Die gesellschaftliche Mitte in Deutschland. Ein Lagebericht*. Frankfurt am Main: Societäts Verlag, pp. 163–226.

Hübinger, Werner (1996): *Prekärer Wohlstand. Neue*

Befunde zu Armut und sozialer Ungleichheit. Freiburg im Breisgau: Lambertus.

Ichheiser, Gustav (1930): *Kritik des Erfolges. Eine soziologische Untersuchung.* Leipzig: Hirschfeld.

Ingham, Geoffrey (1998): "On the Underdevelopment of the Sociology of Money" *Acta Sociologica,* 41(1), 3–18.

Kahneman, Daniel (2011): *Thinking, Fast and Slow.* New York: Farrar, Straus and Giroux.

Kalass, Victoria (2012): *Neue Gewerkschaftskonkurrenz im Bahnwesen. Konflikt um die Gewerkschaft Deutscher Lokomotivführer.* Wiesbaden: Springer VS.

Kaufmann, Franz Xaver (1970): *Sicherheit als soziologisches und sozialpolitisches Problem. Untersuchungen zu einer Wertidee hochdifferenzierter Gesellschaften.* Stuttgart: Enke.

Kierkegaard, Søren (1980): *The Concept of Anxiety: A Simple Psychologically Orienting Deliberation on the Dogmatic Issue of Hereditary Sin.* Edited and translated by Reidar Thomte. Princeton, NJ: Princeton University Press. [*Begrebet Angest,* 1844]

Kirsch, Guy/Mackscheidt, Klaus (1985): *Staatsmann, Demagoge, Amtsinhaber. Eine psychologische Ergänzung der ökonomischen Theorie der Politik.* Göttingen: Vandenhoeck & Ruprecht.

Konrad, Kai (2015): "Affection, Speed Dating and Heartbreaking" *Journal of Popular Economics,* 28(1), 159–72.

Kracauer, Siegfried (1998): *The Salaried Masses: Duty and Distraction in Weimar Germany.* Translated by Quintin Hoare. London: Verso. [*Die Angestellten. Aus dem neuesten Deutschland,* 1929]

Bibliography

Kübler-Ross, Elisabeth (1969): *On Death and Dying.* New York: Macmillan.

Kunkel, Benjamin (2005): *Indecision.* New York: Random House.

Kunkel, Benjamin/Gessen, Keith (eds.) (2008): *Ein Schritt weiter. Die n+1-Anthologie.* Translated by Kevin Vennemann. Frankfurt am Main: Suhrkamp.

Laing, Ronald D./Phillipson, Herbert/Lee, A. Russell (1966): *Interpersonal Perception: A Theory and a Method of Research.* London: Tavistock Publications.

Lasch, Christopher (1979): *The Culture of Narcissism: American Life in An Age of Diminishing Expectations.* New York: W.W. Norton.

Legnaro, Aldo (2004): "Performanz" in Bröckling, Ulrich/Krasmann, Susanne/Lemke, Thomas (eds.): *Glossar der Gegenwart.* Frankfurt am Main: Suhrkamp, pp. 204–9.

Lepsius, Oliver/Meyer-Kalkus, Reinhart (eds.) (2011): *Inszenierung als Beruf. Der Fall Guttenberg.* Berlin: Suhrkamp.

Linden, Michael (2003): "Posttraumatic Embitterment Disorder" *Psychotherapy and Psychosomatics,* 72, 195–202.

Luhmann, Niklas (1989): *Ecological Communication.* Translated by John Bednarz. Cambridge: Polity. [*Ökologische Kommunikation. Kann die moderne Gesellschaft sich auf ökologische Gefährdungen einstellen?,* 1986]

Mau, Steffen (2012): *Lebenschancen. Wohin driftet die Mittelschicht?* Berlin: Suhrkamp.

McCormick, Anne O'Hare (1932): "The two men at the big moment" *New York Times Magazine,* November 6, pp. 1f.

Bibliography

Merton, Robert K. (1968 [1949]): "Contributions to the Theory of Reference Group Behavior" (with Alice S. Rossi) and "Continuities in the Theory of Reference Groups and Social Structure" in Merton, Robert K., *Social Theory and Social Structure*. New York: The Free Press, pp. 279–334 and 335–440.

Mills, C. Wright (2002 [1951]): *White Collar: The American Middle Classes*. Oxford: Oxford University Press.

Minsky, Hyman P. (1982): "The Financial-Instability Hypothesis: Capitalist Processes and the Behavior of the Economy" in Kindleberger, Charles P./Laffargue, Jean-Pierre (eds.): *Financial Crises: Theory, History, and Policy*. Cambridge: Cambridge University Press, pp. 13–47.

Mitscherlich, Margarete (1976 [1972]): "Emanzipation und Sexualität der Frau" in *Müssen wir hassen? Über den Konflikt zwischen innerer und äußerer Realität*. Munich: dtv, pp. 13–53.

Morozov, Evgeny (2013): "Why we are allowed to hate Silicon Valley" *Frankfurter Allgemeine Feuilleton*, November 11, available online at http://www.faz.net/-gqz-7jbae

Münkler, Herfried (2010): *Mitte und Maß. Der Kampf um die richtige Ordnung*. Berlin: Rowohlt.

Neckel, Sighart (2008): *Flucht nach vorn. Die Erfolgskultur der Marktgesellschaft*. Frankfurt am Main: Campus.

Neumann, Franz L. (1957): "Anxiety and Politics" in Marcuse, Herbert (ed.): *The Democratic and the Authoritarian State: Essays in Political and Legal Theory*. Glencoe, IL: The Free Press, pp. 270–300. ["Angst und Politik," 1954]

Bibliography

Oesch, Daniel (2006): *Redrawing the Class Map: Stratification and Institutions in Britain, Germany, Sweden and Switzerland*. Basingstoke: Palgrave Macmillan.

Packard, Vance (1959): *The Status Seekers: An Exploration of Class Behavior in America and the Hidden Barriers that Affect You, Your Community, Your Future*. New York: David McKay.

Parsons, Talcott (1954 [1947]): "Certain Primary Sources and Patterns of Aggression in the Social Structure of the Western World" in *Essays in Sociological Theory*. Glencoe, IL: The Free Press, pp. 298–322.

Pehnt, Annette (2013): *Lexikon der Angst*. Munich: Piper Verlag.

Peters, Birgit (1996): *Prominenz. Eine soziologische Analyse ihrer Entwicklung und Wirkung*. Opladen: Westdeutscher Verlag.

Peuckert, Rüdiger (2008): *Familienformen im sozialen Wandel*. Wiesbaden: VS Verlag.

Popitz, Heinrich (1972): "The Concept of Social Role as an Element of Sociological Theory" in Jackson, John A. (ed.): *Role*. Cambridge: Cambridge University Press, pp. 11–39. [*Der Begriff der sozialen Rolle als Element der soziologischen Theorie*, 1967]

Popitz, Heinrich (2017): *Phenomena of Power: Authority, Domination, and Violence*. Translated by Gianfranco Poggi. New York: Columbia University Press. [*Phänomene der Macht*, 1992]

Postberg, Christian (2013): *Macht und Geld. Über die gesellschaftliche Bedeutung monetärer Verfassungen*. Frankfurt am Main: Campus.

Reich, Robert (1992): *The Work of Nations: Preparing*

Ourselves for 21st-Century Capitalism. New York: Vintage.

Reifner, Udo (2010): *Die Geldgesellschaft. Aus der Finanzkrise lernen*. Wiesbaden: VS Verlag.

Richter, Horst-Eberhard (1972): *Eltern, Kind und Neurose*. Reinbek: Rowohlt.

Riesman, David/Denney, Reuel/Glazer, Nathan (2001 [1950]): *The Lonely Crowd: A Study of the Changing American Character*. New Haven, CT: Yale University Press.

Roosevelt, Franklin D. (1938): "Inaugural Address, March 4, 1933" in Rosenman, Samuel (ed.): *The Public Papers and Addresses of Franklin D. Roosevelt, Volume 2: The Year of Crisis, 1933*. New York: Random House, pp. 11–16.

Runciman, Walter G. (1966): *Relative Deprivation and Social Justice: A Study of Attitudes to Social Inequality in Twentieth-Century England*. London: Routledge & Kegan Paul.

Sahr, Aaron (2017): *Das Versprechen des Geldes: Eine Praxistheorie des Kredits*. Hamburg: Hamburger Edition.

Salter, James (2014): *All That Is*. New York: Vintage International.

Scheler, Max (2010): *Ressentiment*. Translated by Louis A. Coser and William W. Holdheim. Milwaukee, WI: Marquette University Press. [*Das Ressentiment im Aufbau der Moralen*, 1912]

Schörken, Rolf (1984): *Luftwaffenhelfer und Drittes Reich. Die Entstehung eines politischen Bewußtseins*. Stuttgart: Klett-Cotta.

Schultz-Hencke, Harald (1989 [1940]): *Der gehe-*

mmte Mensch. Entwurf eines Lehrbuches der Neo-Psychonanalyse. Stuttgart: Thieme.

Schulz, Hermann/Radebold, Hartmut/Reulecke, Jürgen (2004): *Söhne ohne Väter. Erfahrungen der Kriegsgeneration.* Berlin: Christoph Links Verlag.

Schulz, Walter (1977): "Das Problem der Angst in der neueren Philosophie" in von Ditfurth, Hoimar (ed.): *Aspekte der Angst.* Munich: Kindler, pp. 13–37.

Sennett, Richard (1977): *The Fall of Public Man.* New York: Knopf.

Sennett, Richard (1980): *Authority.* New York: Knopf.

Sennett, Richard (1998): *The Corrosion of Character: The Personal Consequences of Work in the New Capitalism.* New York: W.W. Norton.

Staab, Philipp (2014): *Macht und Herrschaft in der Servicewelt.* Hamburg: Hamburger Edition.

Stack Sullivan, Harry (2001 [1953]): *The Interpersonal Theory of Psychiatry.* London: Routledge.

Stäheli, Urs (2013): "Entnetzt euch! Praktiken und Ästhetiken der Anschlusslosigkeit" *Mittelweg 36*, 22(4), 3–28.

Sternberger, Dolf (1990): "Verfassungspatriotismus" in *Schriften, Bd. X: Verfassungspatriotismus.* Frankfurt am Main: Insel Verlag, pp. 3–16 (first published in *Frankfurter Allgemeine Zeitung*, May 23, 1979, p. 1).

Sullivan, Harry Stack (1997 [1953]): *The Interpersonal Theory of Psychiatry.* New York: W.W. Norton.

Summer, Elisabeth (2008): *Macht die Gesellschaft depressiv? Alain Ehrenbergs Theorie des "erschöpften Selbst" im Licht sozialwissenschaftlicher und therapeutischer Befunde.* Bielefeld: Transcript.

The 2012 Harris Poll Annual RQ Public Summary Report: A Survey of the U.S. General Public Using

the Reputation Quotient," available online at: https://
www.rankingthebrands.com/PDF/The%20reputati
ons%20of%20the%20Most%20Visible%20Compa
nies%202012,%20Harris%20Interactive.pdf

Tillich, Paul (2000 [1952]): *The Courage to Be*. New Haven, CT: Yale University Press.

Tugendhat, Ernst (2016): *Egocentricity and Mysticism: An Anthropological Study*. Translated by Alexei Procyshyn and Mario Wenning. New York: Columbia University Press. [*Egozentrizität und Mystik. Eine anthropologische Studie*, 2003]

Vogl, Joseph (2011): *On Tarrying*. Translated by Helmut Müller-Sievers. London: Seagull Books. [*Über das Zaudern*, 2007]

Watzlawick, Paul/Bavelas Beavin, Janet/Jackson, Don D. (2014 [1967]): *The Pragmatics of Human Communication: A Study of Interactional Patterns, Pathologies, and Paradoxes*. New York: W.W. Norton.

Weber, Max (1978): "Ethnic Groups" in Roth, Guenther/ Wittich, Claus (eds.): *Economy and Society*. Berkeley, CA: University of California Press, pp. 385–398. [*Wirtschaft und Gesellschaft*, 1922]

Wildt, Michael (2009): *An Uncompromising Generation: The Nazi Leadership of the Reich Security Main Office*. Translated by Tom Lampert. Madison, WI: University of Wisconsin Press. [*Generation des Unbedingten. Das Führungskorps des Reichssicherheitshauptamtes*, 2002]

Wilson, Dominic/Dragusanu, Raluca (2008): "The Expanding Middle: The Exploding World Middle Class and Falling Global Inequality" Goldman Sachs Global Economics Paper, No. 170.

Wurmser, Léon (1981): *The Mask of Shame*. Baltimore, MD: Johns Hopkins University Press.

Zacher, Albert (1985): "The Case History and the 'Unlived Life'" in Pichot, P./Berner, P./Wolf, R./Thau, K. (eds.): *Clinical Psychopathology Nomenclature and Classification*. New York: Springer Science+Business Media, pp. 1073–6.

Zuboff, Shoshana (1988): *In the Age of the Smart Machine: The Future of Work and Power*. New York: Basic Books.

Zuboff, Shoshana (2014): "Obama, Merkel, and the Bridge to an Information Civilization" *Frankfurter Allgemeine Zeitung*, January 17, available online at http://www.faz.net/-gqz-7lepg